Comprehensive Healthcare for the U.S.

An Idealized Model

Comprehensive Healthcare for the U.S.

An Idealized Model

WILLIAM F. ROTH, PhD

CRC Press
Taylor & Francis Group
Boca Raton   London   New York

CRC Press is an imprint of the
Taylor & Francis Group, an **informa** business

A PRODUCTIVITY PRESS BOOK

CRC Press
Taylor & Francis Group
6000 Broken Sound Parkway NW, Suite 300
Boca Raton, FL 33487-2742

© 2010 by Taylor and Francis Group, LLC
CRC Press is an imprint of Taylor & Francis Group, an Informa business

No claim to original U.S. Government works

Printed in the United States of America on acid-free paper
10 9 8 7 6 5 4 3 2 1

International Standard Book Number: 978-1-4398-2955-4 (Hardback)

Library of Congress Cataloging-in-Publication Data

Roth, William F.
   Comprehensive healthcare for the U.S. : an idealized model / William F. Roth.
      p. ; cm.
   Includes bibliographical references and index.
   ISBN 978-1-4398-2955-4 (hardcover : alk. paper)
   1. Medical policy--United States. 2. Medical care--United States. 3. Health care reform--United States. I. Title.
   [DNLM: 1. Delivery of Health Care--organization & administration--United States. 2. Comprehensive Health Care--organization & administration--United States. 3. Health Planning--United States. 4. Models, Organizational--United States. W 84 AA1 R845c 2010]

   RA395.A3R675 2010
   362.1'0425--dc22   2009041879

Contents

Preface

During most of my professional career I have worked on design projects. In the Deep South, while part of the poverty program, I helped design one of the first ghetto industries, then one of the first drug education and treatment programs. While in my master's program for social work at the University of Pennsylvania, I helped with a redesign of state mental hospital operations focused on getting the public onto the grounds rather than spilling patients out into the streets (Turning State Mental Hospitals Into Hospital–School Complexes, *Hospital and Community Psychiatry*, March 1978). In my Social Systems Sciences PhD program at The Wharton School, I helped design management systems for small companies, large companies, small communities, cities, and regions.

After graduating, I joined the private sector and was a member of the team that designed a comprehensive quality improvement process for The International Paper Company, one that produced positive bottom line results (*Quality Improvement: A Systems Perspective*, St. Lucie Press, 1998). Then I became a professor and also a Senior Fellow at The Wharton School and worked on a redesign of our education system that freed students to progress at their own rate (Helping Academia Realize Its Potential, *Technos*, July 2000), a design that is now, I am told, being piloted in China. Next, I took part in the development of a new approach to ethics, perhaps helping to come up with the long sought after universal standard (*Ethics In the Workplace: A Systems Perspective*, Pearson Prentice Hall, 2005).

Comprehensive Healthcare for the U.S.: An Idealized Model is about healthcare systems. The initial problem faced in this effort was that I knew almost nothing about healthcare. Fate, however, stepped in, at the last moment, when a colleague could not lead an MBA-level course on healthcare policy and I volunteered to take over. So, there I was with a class of 27 administrators, physicians, physician's assistants, nurses, and nurse practitioners, some with over twenty years experience, whom I was supposed to teach. Thinking quickly, I did what any professor this far in over his or her head would do—I had them teach me.

The challenge laid out was to design a U.S. system that provided comprehensive healthcare for everybody in a cost-effective manner. We started by surveying the systems in countries ranked higher than the U.S. by the 2000 World Health Organization study to discover their strengths. We contacted physicians in these countries to elaborate on what we had learned. Then, we incorporated these strengths into a model for the United States, adding some ideas of our own. This went on through six sessions of the course, three years, fourteen countries, hundreds of articles and books, tons of phone calls and e-mails abroad. More than eighty professionals from this country and others contributed, doing all of the research and some of the writing.

I obviously cannot thank each one of these people personally, but two of my DeSales University MBA students stand out. Maria Gardell kept pushing in the early days, did a great deal of research, and wrote part of the first draft of the chapter on education. Art Leibeinguth did the initial research for and completed a first draft of the chapter on information systems. I would also like to thank Dr. Yukako Sugiura for helping me understand the Japanese healthcare system, it strengths and weaknesses; Dr. George Saj, a college friend, who has kept me up-to-date on the arguments of those opposed to universal healthcare, or to changes in our current system; and John Kalish, my childhood friend, a long-time resident of Brussels who helped me understand the direction in which Western European nations are moving.

Once again, many thanks go to these people and to everybody who contributed to this effort. I hope that our work can help make a difference.

1

Introduction

THE CHALLENGE

In today's world, healthcare is provided in one of two ways. Most developed countries provide it free. Either the required attention itself is free—one simply goes to the doctor without any exchange of cash—or one pays for it with free insurance provided by the government. Such systems are obviously not-for-profit. The second alternative is for healthcare to be part of the for-profit sector. In such systems, people pay for services either out of their own pockets or, more likely, using private insurance provided by their employer. In the latter case, at least part of the payments for policy premiums is generated through payroll deductions.

Both approaches have weaknesses. Major concerns with the not-for-profit approach include administrative costs, over-usage, lack of incentive for people to go into the healthcare field, lack of innovation and development. Of these, over-usage is probably the most serious. Major concerns in for-profit systems include lack of service for people unable to pay personally or through insurance, unequal service for different population segments, unreasonable costs resulting from the greed factor, and inefficiencies arising from redundancies. (Just how many computed axial tomography scanner machines do we need in one town?)

In for-profit societies in the world, over-usage is less of a problem than in the not-for-profit situation, but frequently for the wrong reasons. Lack of incentive is also less of a problem as well as lack of innovativeness and development. In not-for-profit societies, however, lack of service is not a problem, and unequal service should not be a problem if the system is set up correctly, cost is not a problem for the individual, and is less of a problem for governments if the system is organized correctly. Inefficiencies/redundancies should, again, not be a problem if the system is set up correctly.

In the United States, the argument between these two camps has raged nonstop for some time. Both sides have strong points. Both sides, however, tend to get buried in the details and lose sight of the central issue, which is: Should healthcare be a right or a privilege?

Our answer to this question is based on the realization that the most important indicator of any modern society's success is its ability to develop and effectively utilize the potential of its citizens. If one looks around the world, one realizes that countries doing the best are those where the population has access to comprehensive education; where people are able to improve themselves economically through work that, at the same time, contributes to the welfare of society as a whole; and where a system of governance exists that encourages individual as well as societal development.

Certain inputs are absolutely necessary to development of the population's potential. Access to education, as we have said, is one. Part of the reason Great Britain lost her empire was that education remained for too long a privilege available only to the upper classes, while, across the channel and the ocean, it had become a right of all citizens. Healthcare is another necessary input. It is extremely difficult to develop ones potential fully when one is constantly worrying about injury or illness, when one is constantly worrying about how to gain medical attention or about how to pay for it.

The two major problems with the for-profit approach are lack of access and lack of equitable treatment. As long as the profit motive continues to drive our healthcare system, these problems are not going to disappear. If the major objective of those involved, specifically practitioners, insurance companies, and pharmaceutical companies, is to make as much money as possible no matter what the cost to society, treating those who cannot pay is an unattractive distraction. This attitude is not going to change. A large and powerful segment of our population, a segment generally labeled "conservative," believes that it should not. They believe that "free enterprise," with the profit motive as its foundation, lies at the root of our nation's economic success.

This most likely is true, at least up to this point. At the same time, however, because a growing majority of citizens believe strongly, and from a pragmatic rather than an idealistic perspective, that healthcare must be a *right* of all citizens in any country hoping to thrive in the modern world, we would suggest that our healthcare system needs, if it is to become effective and universal, to shed the trapping and shortcomings of free enterprise. The for-profit approach has had its chance. And though it has produced some benefits, when one adopts an overall perspective and compares it to other approaches in place, it has failed. It has not been able to overcome its weaknesses. In fact, these weaknesses seem currently to be growing worse, attempts to fix them patchwork style, attempts at improvement only exacerbating the situation.

Opponents of universal healthcare, of course, immediately begin shouting *SOCIALISM*. Yes, it is socialism; it is definitely socialism we are talking about. But, those same shouters refuse to realize that the United States has been practicing economic socialism since the early 1900s.

Opponents will say that such a system kills incentive. With this we must disagree. No, it doesn't. It is *communism* as an economic approach that kills incentive. Communism is when everybody works as hard as they can, generating as much wealth as possible, all the wealth generated then being poured into a common pot and distributed according to need. Very idealistic, but the problem is that people want to benefit according to their individual efforts and eventually become frustrated. The result of this frustration is that they stop trying.

The laissez-faire approach or "free enterprise," at the other end of the economic spectrum, kills competition rather than incentive. In this system, people work as hard as they can and keep whatever they make, putting it to whatever use they wish. No regulations are enforced, the government remains uninvolved, a "law of the jungle" atmosphere prevailing.

In the United States, we had laissez-faire in the late 1800s and early 1900s. Within a period of fifty years, approximately twenty of the most ruthless, the most driven industrialists, a group eventually labeled the "Robber Barons" took over our entire economy and ran it to benefit themselves, doing whatever necessary to discourage competition. Again, today, after the easing of government regulation under Reagan, Clinton, and Bush Jr., we are experiencing a taste of laissez-faire, with huge fortunes being amassed on Wall Street and by top corporate executives while the rest of us suffer.

Socialism is everything in between the communism and laissez-faire ends of the spectrum. We all work as hard as we can to generate wealth. The government takes a percentage of what we earn to support public services necessary to the development of individual potential—services like healthcare, education, police, and the military. There are presently no pure communist economies left in the world, no pure laissez-faire economies left either. The only remaining question concerning a country's economic approach is where on the socialism scale does it lie. How much of everybody's paycheck is taken? How many services are provided in exchange for that money?

DEALING WITH THE WEAKNESSES

If we do decide that healthcare should be a right rather than a privilege and adopt a truly universal healthcare system (UHS) approach, how do we deal with the previously mentioned weaknesses of a not-for-profit approach? For example, does a way exist to introduce the strengths of the for-profit system into a not-for-profit system? Is it possible, maybe, to combine the two in some manner so that we come up with a more effective hybrid? What can we learn from other cultures that have versions of what we are attempting to design already in place? Finally, and perhaps most importantly, rather than just patching or rearranging the parts of the traditional model, can we view the challenge from a different perspective, and can we generate entirely new solutions for old problems?

For example, in order to deal with the problem of over-usage, most countries have depended on the decisions of doctors, facility administrators, and government administrators. We believe that they have been looking through the wrong end of the telescope. They are thinking in the traditional top-down manner. The patient, actually, should be the prime actor. Is it possible to give citizens an incentive to cut down on visits while, at the same time, meeting their healthcare needs?

The contributors to this book have taken all of the above into consideration in their effort to design an idealized version of a universal healthcare system that not only realizes the importance of total coverage, but also takes into account the cost and the strengths and weaknesses of our culture.

When we say "idealized," we are indicating that our approach will differ from that of Governor Romney in Massachusetts, of Governor Schwarzenegger in California, of Senator Clinton, and, finally, of President Obama. All of these people have begun with the current system, identified its shortcomings and tried to correct at least some of them. The objective of our approach will be, rather, to design a "perfect" model that will act as a "target" to aim for when we begin redesigning the parts, when we begin identifying and prioritizing improvements. The change process will become easier and more meaningful when we know where we want to end up, enabling us to pick those projects that get us the farthest along our path the fastest.

In summation, the purpose of this book is to design an "idealized" universal healthcare system for the United States that ensures every citizen access to adequate treatment in the most cost-effective manner possible. Our effort will be systemic, which means that we will not focus on one part of the system at a time. We will not do so due to our realization that interactions between the parts are just as important to success as the parts themselves. For example, we cannot address the current rapidly rising cost of healthcare without taking into account the education system, the amount of money pharmaceutical companies spend on advertising, the politicizing of decisions that affect the healthcare realm. No problem stands alone. To approach problems as though they do, indeed, stand alone, frequently produces more damage than good.

Rather than focusing on individual parts, we shall begin by focusing on the *whole*; we shall begin by defining the characteristics we believe that an "ideal" healthcare system should possess *as a whole*. Then, we shall try to design these characteristics into what we consider to be the most critical parts of that system. The ideal characteristics of the model we intend to create, based on our belief that healthcare should be a right, need to include:

- Prevention as the major focus
- Universal, free coverage available for preventative and basic healthcare
- Steadily increasing cost effectiveness
- Increasingly efficient use of healthcare system resources
- Nonpoliticized government involvement due to the need for the system to be supported by tax revenues
- Customer education as an integral and primary role of the system
- Quality of care improving continually
- Most advanced technology available to all
- Ongoing, high-quality research in all areas
- Free or affordable training for all healthcare professionals that is on-going

- Free health-related pharmaceuticals for all citizens
- Effective use of all involved professionals in providing healthcare
- The design of a healthcare facility network that allows universal access
- A national, easily accessible data system that stores patient information and facilitates research
- An equitable, national taxing structure that pays for the system including patient care, research, professional education, and facilities
- Protection for professionals from debilitating law suits
- Choice between the UHS and a private healthcare sector

By definition, of course, an "ideal" is unreachable. But, this is not important because, as systems thinkers say, it is what happens, what we learn during the journey that is most important. Also, it is understood that what we define as an ideal this week might not be ideal next week, the only absolute in life being "change," so that our ideal will necessarily continue to evolve as we pursue it.

The critical parts of our "idealized" model, those that will have our ideal characteristics designed into them, include:

1. A nonpoliticized hierarchy of governing boards of directors including representatives from all major stakeholder groups (including government).
2. A nonpoliticized hierarchy of Departments of Administration.
3. A panel of experts (not just lawyers) given the power to arbitrate complaints against healthcare professionals including malpractice and to decide financial rewards. The right for patients to appeal the panel's decisions.
4. A network of community health centers staffed by physicians, physician's assistants, nurses, nurse practitioners, social workers, and therapists; the centers providing satellite services and feeding into specialized clinics, general hospitals, and teaching/research hospitals.
5. Extensive use of vans, hot lines, and telemedicine as part of community health center satellite services to provide preventative education and to cover the needs of patients at home and living in rural communities.
6. A network of nursing homes.
7. A set fee for each service delivered defined by the National Board of Directors.

8. A government-allotted allowance covering individual payment for UHS services, citizens being allowed to keep part of what is left at the end of the year as an incentive to stay healthy.
9. A catastrophic fund to cover patients who use up their yearly allowance.
10. An incentive system for UHS teams that encourages preventative care and efficient treatment.
11. Private insurance that can be bought as a supplement to the UHS allowance by those who want services deemed not necessary (e.g., cosmetic surgery) or for those who simply prefer the private sector for treatment. Doctors and their teams can work for the UHS or in the private sector financed by private insurance, but they cannot work in both. Patients can use either or both.
12. Government investment in pharmaceutical research to compensate for caps on the prices of prescription drugs.
13. A universal information system built on standards that ensure the ability of all parts to communicate and that link all parts through centralized storage "nodes."
14. Free education for healthcare personnel repaid at least in part through community service.

Russell L. Ackoff, who along with Peter Drucker and W. Edwards Deming comprise the trinity of modern-day management theory, said the following during a recent interview.

> … our healthcare system is a mess. We are the only developed country in the world without universal coverage; about 42 million people are uninsured. It is estimated that excessive testing, excessive surgery, or excessive prescribing of drugs that interact adversely causes at least half of the illness in the U.S. The federal government recently found that about one million people per year are seriously infected while in hospitals and approximately 100,000 die from these infections. *The fact is that the U.S. doesn't have a healthcare system.* We have an illness and disability care system. Why? We, or our surrogates, pay the system for taking care of us when we are sick or disabled. Therefore, the greatest threat to the existence of the system is pervasive health! Little wonder that the system accepts and encourages practices that preserve, maintain and create illness and disabilities.

The time has come for somebody to see the real problem and say, "Let's design a healthcare system, one that has incentives for producing and maintaining health, not illness and disabilities."[1]

That has become the mission of our group, to design a healthcare system that has incentives for producing and maintaining health. In order for our presentation to make sense, however, we first need to examine the strengths and weaknesses of our current system. It is important to make absolutely clear why change is needed.

REFERENCE

1. Russell L. Ackoff, Iconoclastic Management Authority, Advocates a 'Systemic' Approach to Innovation, Robert J. Allio, *Strategy and Leadership*, 31(3), 2003, 19–26.

2

The Current U.S. Healthcare "Mess"

THE CHALLENGE

In systems terminology, a "mess" is a system of interdependent problems that feed off each other. In terms of the U.S. healthcare system, the "mess" is gigantic, a multiheaded hydra that affects every aspect of our lives. And like the hydra, while we are battling one of its heads, several others are sneaking around behind to bite us in the rear.

Isolating and dealing with healthcare system problems one at a time has never worked and never will work, though this has been our traditional approach. We have not ventured beyond this approach because trying to wrap our arms around an entire mess of this magnitude is a daunting task; a never-ending series of crises force us to focus our attention and resources on the parts since both practitioners and patients usually have a limited span of interest. Researchers working on a cancer breakthrough, for example, are not too interested in why the staffs of intercity free clinics have such rapid turnover. But, still, an overview of the mess we are attempting to address is necessary if we are to develop a comprehensive, useful approach to unraveling it.

Symptoms of the "illness" in our healthcare system are easy to uncover. Most of us know by this time that our country spends nearly twice as much per capita on healthcare as any other nation in the world, and that, while in 1970, 7 percent of our gross domestic product (GDP) went for healthcare, this figure rose to 13 percent in 1999 and to 16 percent in 2008. The projection is that, if a drastic change does not occur, this figure will reach 19.5 percent by the year 2017; the percentage being spent on health-care in the United States again is close to double that being spent in other developed countries.[1]

Most of us also know that in the year 2001 the World Health Organization (WHO) ranked the United States thirty-seventh among the 191 member nations in terms of the overall quality of our healthcare system. All European nations were ahead of us. France ranked first that year, Italy second, Spain seventh, Great Britain eighteenth, Sweden twenty-third, and Germany twenty-fifth.

Canada, our neighbor, ranked thirtieth, while Japan ranked tenth, Colombia twenty-second, and Morocco twenty-ninth. Though this information was released nine years ago and rankings have not been broadcast for the following years, it should still be a call to action. Criteria used to establish this ranking included the country's ability to make "the health status of the entire population as good as possible"; the country's ability to respond to people's expectations; and the country's ability to ensure financial protection for all, the involved cost being distributed according to the population's ability to pay.

Those defending our current system, or course, dispute the use of these criteria. Why, for example, is quality of care not the major focus? To me, however, the criteria are pretty much on target. Until care is available, quality can't be a consideration, at least to those who lack access to care. At the same time, if care is made available, but remains unaffordable, then, again, the quality of services provided to those able to pay for it doesn't really matter to those unable to pay. Getting the basics—availability and affordability—in place has to be our No. 1 priority. Even more damning is the fact that the WHO survey ranked the United States seventy-second in terms of our population's overall level of health. [2]

At the same time, most of us know that while a small but extremely vocal group continues to claim that the U.S. healthcare system has always been and remains "the best in the world," that it just needs a little bit of fine tuning, a growing majority, approximately 80 percent of our population, are saying that comprehensive healthcare should be a right, and that some sort of universal healthcare system most definitely needs to be put into place.

So, let's see. Our society offers the most expensive healthcare in the world while receiving low grades for the way it is delivered. A large majority of the public is calling for drastic reform, but, in actuality, little is changing—baby steps at best.

Something is obviously wrong, something is very wrong, indeed. And, yet, as we have said, very little has changed over the past decade. Small patches have been applied here and there. A bill has recently been passed by the U.S. Congress insuring children whose families cannot afford private insurance, but make too much to be eligible for Medicaid. Veteran benefits are being expanded. The outcry over executive salaries in the healthcare insurance industry is growing. But these are, indeed, just patches. Very little has been attempted in terms of improving our situation as a whole since the Clinton's effort during the 1990s was sabotaged by special interests.

The question that obviously comes to mind at this point is: But, why has so little been done? U.S. citizens currently spend close to $2.5 trillion yearly on healthcare through direct payments, salary deductions, or corporate contributions. They spend this money on a system that, as a whole, apparently does not provide the services it is supposed to provide on the scale expected of them. An article in the December 1, 2008, *Washington Post* claimed that "as much as half of the 2.3 trillion spent today does nothing to improve health"; a pretty stunning indictment that, if true, is also a startling cry for change.[3]

The question, therefore, must be asked again: Why hasn't change occurred? At the same time, an even more important question that needs to be addressed once the first one has been answered is: What can we do *to make change occur; how can we force it?*

But let's start with the "why hasn't change occurred?"

In order to understand a mess, we need first to identify the individual problems that make up its web. The individual problems that have been identified thus far in the U.S. healthcare realm include:

1. Healthcare sector policy at the federal level.
2. The effects of the profit motive on the delivery of healthcare including the resultant lack of integration between programs and services, but especially between the medical records systems of these programs and services.
3. The involvement of insurance companies as the middleman, the increased bureaucracy, the increased cost, and the resultant misuse of healthcare professionals' time.

4. The cost of prescription drugs.
5. The cost to professionals of legal protection and of malpractice suits.
6. People not taking care of themselves; people not seeking preventative care and early treatment.
7. The cost of education for healthcare professionals.

Again, we realize that none of these problems stands alone, that they feed off each other, exacerbate each other, often creating new problems. But, let's start by first trying to develop an understanding of at least several of the individual core problems before addressing their interactions.

Policy Issues

Historically, the focus of U.S. healthcare has differed from that of countries with systems considered superior to ours. As Dr. Lawrence Brown claims in his *New England Journal of Medicine* article, since the National Institutes of Health began taking national healthcare policy seriously some 60 years ago in the United States, those making decisions in the United States have paid the most attention to research and to the development of cures for disease, while in other countries the focus has been on securing the citizenry's access to care.[4]

In order to realize this priority, the other countries developed some form of a universal healthcare system (UHS), financed mainly through taxes, that provided all services for all sectors and all ages. This care has been delivered either for no charge at the time of payment (with the exception of a small co-pay), in exchange for government-provided insurance that covers the fee and is handled electronically, or for immediate payment by the patient who then is reimbursed by the government.

In most of these countries, citizens also have access to supplemental private insurance that covers things not covered by the UHS. This insurance gives the subscriber, in some cases, access to a higher quality of service. The private insurance is made available by employers or bought out-of-pocket.

The breakdown between government funds (tax) and private funds spent on healthcare in countries with a UHS is approximately 70 percent to 30 percent, respectively.[5] In this scenario, the cost of private insurance is definitely held down by competition, but not so much by competition between the individual private insurance firms. Rather, it is held down by competition between private sector offerings and the government-supported universal coverage. People can turn without cost to the latter if they are not satisfied with private sector prices or service.

As we have seen, in contrast, the U.S. system has grown into a hodge-podge of often competing, poorly integrated services.

Approximately 44 percent of our public healthcare spending is financed by tax revenues. These government-provided funds are used mainly to support five different major government programs serving five different segments of the population.

Medicare

This program currently covers 45 million Americans age 65 and over along with some disabled citizens not over 65. It is paid for with federal income tax revenues and payroll taxes. Enrollee co-pays are necessary for some services. In 2008, Medicare accounted for approximately one-fifth of our total national spending on personal healthcare.[6] Things not covered by Medicare include dental, hearing, and vision, the organs that tend to go first as we age, forcing those who cannot afford supplemental insurance to pay out of pocket or to go without, unless they can get Medicaid or the VA to contribute. Neither pay for preventative services.

People eligible for Medicare end up spending approximately 20 percent of their income on healthcare, making up the difference between what Medicare pays and the actual cost.[7] That is a negative. A positive is that, in terms of the big picture, the single-payer approach used by Medicare makes this system much more efficient administratively, much cheaper overall to run than private systems.

Medicaid

This program provides government-sponsored healthcare for poor children, for their parents, and for the disabled. If an adult does not have a child, however, no matter how poor he or she might be, that person does not qualify.[8] Federal and state taxes pay for Medicaid.

Individual states decide the level of income necessary for eligibility. States also have been given responsibility for administering Medicaid so that there are fifty different programs in the country at this point with little integration of efforts.

A major problem is that Medicaid patients are frequently rejected by providers due to the low level of reimbursement offered by the program. Most of these people cannot afford to add anything out of pocket and, therefore, are forced to seek other alternatives or to go without.

Veteran's Administration

This program cares for veterans through its own network of hospitals and clinics. Federal tax dollars fund it. Treatment is either free or extremely affordable.

Tricare

This is a federal program designed to cover active duty members of the military and their families with federally funded insurance similar to that offered by private insurance companies.

SCHIP

A fairly new program started in 1997, SCHIP (State Children's Health Insurance Program) provides free health-related services for children whose parents cannot afford private insurance, but make too much to qualify for Medicaid. The parents of these children, however, are not covered. SCHIP is funded by a combination of federal and state taxes.

So, in the United States on the public side, we have five independent programs providing free or mostly free services to four separate populations. Each program has its own bureaucracy, its own information system and store of data, its own policies, and its own budget. Minimal communication occurs between the five.

Then, in the United States, we have the private sector that includes the previously discussed for-profit and not-for-profit insurance companies. Premiums in this sector are paid by employers and employees, the employer usually paying the most. In the case of the self-employed, the unemployed, the retired but not yet eligible for Medicare, and those too wealthy to qualify for Medicaid, the premium is paid out-of-pocket. When the individual is the sole payer, insurance companies have the right to deny coverage based on preexisting conditions, thus the patient must pay for medical attention completely out-of-pocket until he or she is poor enough to quality for Medicaid.

Obviously, our healthcare system has evolved with less than the necessary amount of planning, with no real overview, with no clearly defined set of objectives, and with more emphasis on research and treatment than on prevention. As Dr. Donald Berwick, president of the Institute for Healthcare Improvement, said, "We wait for people to get sick, and then we invest enormous sums to fix them up."[9]

Does this make sense? I don't believe so, not in terms of the overall health and productivity of our population, not in terms of cost. Prevention is obviously cheaper than treatment. Research and new cures are certainly important, but it might be more important to focus primarily on keeping people from becoming ill in the first place. Healthcare policy in other developed countries makes prevention one of its cornerstones. We might be able to learn something from these countries, especially after we wean our system from the profit motive, especially after we decide that comprehensive healthcare in the United States should become a right rather than a privilege.

One more extremely important point that people don't seem cognizant of should be clarified while we are discussing government policy. Opponents of a universal system, obviously led by those profiting the most from our current fragmented one, claim that it would increase cost tremendously; that a ponderous, expensive new government bureaucracy would need to be created; that the American taxpayer would suffer the additional cost; that too much is going on now; that the medical community is too busy to risk making a change at this point.[10]

These people are ignoring the facts or are making them up as they go along. Concerning additional cost, it has been pointed out repeatedly in the literature, as we have said, that the United States now pays roughly twice as much per capita for healthcare as any other country. This means that if we go universal, if we are willing to learn from countries that provide better overall service, if we are willing to make the necessary changes, we could provide comprehensive healthcare for our entire population for roughly one-half the current cost to taxpayers, or for approximately the same amount now being spent on our public programs. As we have said, 45 percent of healthcare-dedicated tax revenues are currently being spent on Medicare, Medicaid, the VA, Tricare, and SCHIP. If our UHS is designed correctly, this amount could cover *everyone* rather than just select segments of our population.

Concerning the expense of a new, ponderous government bureaucracy, let's see. We now have a bureaucracy running Medicare, a separate bureaucracy running Medicaid, a separate bureaucracy running the Veterans Administration, a separate bureaucracy running SCHIP, as well as the large bureaucratic function required of each insurance company, the cost of this function being paid for by taxes or written into premium charges.

In countries with UHS, one bureaucracy frequently handles all the administrative matters for the entire country, or for each province, as in Canada. Economies of scale come into play when we go big. Instead of five people doing the same thing in five different locations, we have four people working together in one location, or three people in one location. Economies of standardization come into play. Instead of five or more different sets of policies to follow, five or more different sets of forms to fill out, we have one. The decrease in the amount of paperwork would be great.

The administrative costs of Medicare, handled by a large government bureaucracy, are apparently less that 2 percent of the whole, while those of private, for-profit hospitals average around 34 percent.[11] If we can spread the Medicare system or something similar to it through the entire healthcare network, the savings in terms of cost, time, mistakes, and increased customer satisfaction should be obvious.

Concerning the claim that the healthcare sector is too busy to risk change, if an athlete realizes in the middle of a close game that he or she has broken a leg, does that person say, "Sorry, I'm too busy now to take care of it." Of course not. The athlete's realization is that if nothing is done the leg will just keep getting worse. The "too busy" explanation is nothing more than an illogical, weak rationalization for blocking change.

But, then we need to ask, "If the arguments against change are so weak, why have the opponents of UHS been so successful?"

This book, as we have said, is written from a systems perspective. In systems terminology, a "mess," as we have said, is a web of interdependent problems that feed off of one another. One of the important parts in the healthcare web is Congress. Politicians in the U.S. Congress can be and frequently are bought, not so much because they are corrupt, but because it costs so much to run a campaign and to get elected. Currently, for example, running for a seat in the House of Representatives costs roughly between $500,000 and $1,000,000 in contributions.

Quite simply, those who benefit from stopping change in the healthcare system contribute a portion of their profits to campaigns; they spend a portion of their profits to buy votes. Until this changes, until limits are put on the size of campaign chests or until those in favor of UHS begin bettering the contributions offered candidates by the opposition, little of what we are talking about in this book is going to happen. This is a sad fact, but true.

The amount of political freedom we enjoy in this nation is one of our greatest strengths. But, also, at the same time, it can be one of our most debilitating weaknesses.

The Profit Motive

The profit motive and the competition it inspires lie at the core of a free enterprise economic system. The theory is that competition between organizations keeps prices in check due to the law of supply and demand, allowing customers to get the best deal. There is, of course, also a downside to the involved competition. In a competitive environment every business has to set up its own operation, buy its own equipment, organize its own distributorship, do its own advertising; these costs being factored into the price charged for goods and services produced.

The cost for U.S. healthcare is covered in the following manner (these figures, of course, change constantly, but should be in the general range):

22 percent out of pocket
5 percent individually paid for private insurance
27 percent employment-based private insurance
43 percent government financing
3 percent private and philanthropic funds[12]

Healthcare spending grew 5.7 percent faster than the overall U.S. economy last year. A primary cause identified for these increases is the profits taken by private health insurance companies as well as administrative costs created by the interaction of these companies with healthcare practitioners, healthcare organizations, and government agencies involved in healthcare. In 2002, these costs reached 19 to 24 percent of the total here as compared to 11 percent of the total in Canada.

Another thing that increases cost, of course, is the services rendered— the technology used to provide that service, how long a person stays in the hospital, how many doctors are seen. Because of the way insurance companies pay—the more services provided, the more the physician earns—doctors tend to order more tests than are necessary. Also, in order to protect themselves against malpractice suits, an important source of profit for lawyers, doctors are forced to take every possible precaution, practicing what is called "defensive medicine."

These incentives, of course, increase the size of the bill sent to the insurance company that, in turn, passes the additional charges on to the consumer in the form of raised premiums so that it can maintain its own profit margin.

An important point needs to be taken into consideration when talking about the profit motive and the competition resulting from it. This is the difference between a *right* and a *privilege*. Free enterprise is based on the belief that sellers should charge as much as possible for what they are selling, that people should be willing to earn the things they purchase through work. This makes sense in the realm of *privileges* (what kind of car you drive, what kind of house you live in, how you dress, what you eat). But it doesn't work well in the realm of *rights*. In this instance, saying that people must earn the required healthcare is illogical; that if they aren't able to do so, no matter how hard they try, too bad. Excluding people from such services to any degree is hurting not only them, but the country as a whole due to lost productivity, due to the cost incurred supporting this populace through our different forms of welfare.

Unfortunately, a lot of "free enterprise thinking" and competition exists within the U.S. healthcare industry. While this competition used to be between individual hospitals, it is now between "healthcare networks" including hospitals, specialized clinics, and practices of different sizes and shapes. In my community, for example, three large networks are battling it out, gobbling up everything they can. Both want to be the biggest and the best in every area, purchasing all of the most sophisticated technology available with no desire to share, to coordinate efforts, with no desire to develop complementary specializations.

The amount of money wasted in this country through the unnecessary overlap of technology and services would be difficult to estimate, but it must, indeed, be large. And, then, there is the advertising budget made necessary by competition, a relatively small amount, but still another cost.

The alternative, of course, is to develop a well-integrated healthcare system where facilities specialize and patients are sent to the one housing the most appropriate technology and skills. If the objective is to provide comprehensive, cost-effective healthcare for the entire population, this cooperative, integrated approach would seem to make more sense than the competitive one we now have in place.

Another problem with our competitive approach to healthcare is the desire to cut costs whenever and wherever possible, a strategy that frequently backfires. An example would be one of the network builders in our community who had orderlies and other lower level employees take over nursing duties so he could get rid of the higher paid, professional nurses in order to save on their salaries. Patients, of course, began complaining, customers started going to the competition, and eventually the hospital had to deal with the additional expense of hiring and training a new crew of nurses, most of the original staff refusing to return.

Again concerning competition and its negative effects on the efficiency of healthcare, the lifeblood of any such system is information. It is necessary for diagnosis, for effective treatment, for research, for practitioner learning, for management. It is critical to the survival of the organization. In the United States, due to the competitive environment, most healthcare networks have their own information system in place, their own technology, with no desire to share technology when sharing would cut costs. Quite frequently, the systems in place are from different dealers and don't even talk to each other, so the organizations do not share the data and information generated, which is another lost efficiency, another lost opportunity to improve treatment, another increase in cost.

The alternative is to have a centralized information system similar to that found in most Western European countries, one that all healthcare facilities feed into and have access to, even across borders. Efforts are apparently being made in the United States to move in this direction, but the competitive environment remains a hindrance.

On the treatment level, the profit motive, as it now is put into play in this country, encourages the wrong thing if our objective is to provide comprehensive healthcare for everybody. Quite simply, people do what they are rewarded for doing. If professionals in the medical industry were rewarded for stressing prevention, they would stress prevention.

I have a healthcare insurance policy from a major provider sitting in front of me on my desk that says the company will pay nothing for preventative treatment. The rationalization involved is that people might take advantage of a focus on prevention, might try to be paid for taking walks. The truth of the matter, of course, is that the profit is not in prevention. Quite simply, if everybody got healthy, the companies would sell less insurance.

Doctors, as well, are caught in the profit trap. They are paid much more, as we have said, for curing people than for keeping them from getting sick. As a result, there are far too many unnecessary surgeries, far too many situations where doctors keep seeing patients who don't have anything wrong with them, but who just like the attention. And, there are far too many faulty diagnoses because the doctor is in a hurry to see as many patients as possible; the average appointment lasting, from what I have been told, around twelve minutes.

Changing the reward system to focus on prevention, shifting the profit from cure to prevention would be a relatively simple challenge. Most countries with a universal healthcare system have done so, or are moving in that direction. What is being said is not that the profit motive is bad. It can produce excellent results if utilized in the proper manner. What is being said is that we need to design a system that does, indeed, utilize it in the proper manner and that uses it to encourage the right things.

In summation, while competition driven by the profit motive might produce some positive results in the healthcare sector, the negative results currently produced are far more costly, both in terms of treatment and the bottom line. When trying to deliver something that should be a *right* for all citizens, rather than a *privilege* earned only by those who can afford it, cooperation is generally more effective. At the same time we are saying that the profit motive at this point is pushing us in the wrong direction, but, with some rethinking and redesign, could become a powerful tool in helping us achieve our objective.

Healthcare Insurance

Private insurance companies act as the middleman in a majority of for-profit healthcare sector transactions and nonprofit healthcare sector transactions that do not involve government programs. Insurance companies are for-profit, bureaucratic organizations trying to make as much money as possible, living or dying by their bottom line. According to a 2007 Kaiser Family Foundation study, between 2001 and 2008, premiums for family coverage have increased 78 percent while wages have risen approximately 20 percent, the worker paying approximately 27 percent of the cost out-of-pocket.[13] It is estimated that more than 30 percent of every dollar spent in the United States for healthcare services goes to insurance companies for administrative costs, part of this money ending up in multimillion dollar executive salaries and bonuses.[14]

And what do insurance companies do to earn their 30 percent? They take money from payees and distribute it to those providing the service, something that can now be done more effectively by technology if the right system is put into place and the right safeguards are instituted to protect the payee.

In terms of the competition among insurance companies that supposedly holds costs down, little actually exists. Because several giants dominate the market, price ranges can tacitly be agreed upon and set without anything being said or signed. At the same time, the use of insurance as a means of transferring funds requires that a bureaucracy be established in the hospital, clinic, or practice to deal with the paperwork. It has been estimated that healthcare professionals spend up to 40 percent of their time completing the necessary paperwork, depriving patients of treatment, thus depriving the organization of income.

Next, because insurance is the main vehicle for accessing treatment when individual or families are not eligible for Medicare, Medicaid, VA benefits, Tricare, or SCHIP, and because approximately 47 million citizens do not have such insurance (for a number of reasons), these people tend to forgo preventative and early treatment and wait until the ailment grows serious or debilitating. By waiting, it will cost a lot more to deal with, not only in terms of treatment, but also in terms of lost hours on the job and government-provided support (unemployment, welfare, food stamps, etc.).

Finally, insurance companies are notorious for taking decisions concerning "what treatment the patient needs" (translates to: "what we are willing to pay for") away from the doctor and for dictating the amount and type of information required to gain reimbursement. If the doctor fights, the fight again takes time away from his or her main responsibilities. If the patient joins the battle, it takes even more time on both ends. In fact, most insurance companies have an entire department dedicated to dealing with such attacks. This is another major expense that customers end up paying for.

Quite simply, the main mission of insurance companies, as we have said, is to make as much profit as possible, rather than to do what is best for the people served. This means that they raise their premiums as frequently as possible, that they pay out as little as possible for treatments, and that they frequently pay out nothing for prevention, which ends up costing the rest of the healthcare system a lot more than it should.

Cost of Prescription Drugs

Everybody knows that we pay more for pharmaceuticals than any other country. We have all heard about prescriptions costing several hundred dollars a week, about people being forced to choose between groceries and being able to afford their medications. We have all heard that the United States is the largest consumer of pharmaceuticals, accounting for approximately 50 percent of the global market, that our consumption level continues to increase while the price of pharmaceuticals continues to rise. In fact, according to testimony before the Senate Finance Committee cited in *Families USA* (April 2004), the cost of pharmaceuticals is rising faster than that of other component of healthcare. This same article cites Budget Office estimates that senior citizens with average pharmaceutical expenses who live at the median income level will see this expenditure rise from 8.8 percent of their income in 2006 to 12.3 percent in 2013. That is an almost 30 percent increase with no end to the upward trend in sight.[15]

Why are drugs more expensive in this country than others? One reason is that the profit margins in the industry are among the highest. The rationalization for these margins offered by pharmaceutical companies is, quite simply, that the profits are deserved. Drugs help save the taxpayer a great deal of money by preventing diseases that keep people home from work, that put people in the hospital. They say that drugs help keep older people healthy, thus cutting Medicare expenses, that drugs help keep people free from debilitating diseases that make them dependent for survival on Medicaid and welfare.

The counter argument to this rationalization, of course, is that drugs have the same effect in other countries where pharmaceutical companies don't make such huge profits.

Drug companies say they sponsor programs that provide free or lower cost drugs for those who cannot afford them. Thus, we have another bureaucracy, this one saddled with the responsibility of figuring out whether a family can or cannot afford the cost, saddled with the responsibility of deciding where to draw the line, a task made almost impossible by the number of variables that need to be taken into account. Such programs, of course, are mainly public relations, part of the company's efforts to generate the image of being community- as well as profit-oriented. But profit, obviously, remains the major objective, so that those applying are frequently forced to jump through a number of hoops in order to gain this service.

A second reason offered by pharmaceutical companies to explain high prices is the cost of research. They complain that they are being forced to charge more for their products in the United States because of the price caps in other countries, that the money lost abroad has to be made up here in order to support research and development. The United States does, indeed, carry out more research than any other country, approximately 20 percent more, and does, indeed, produce an ever-expanding range of drugs that help keep people alive longer and in a healthier state.

But the argument about the higher prices being necessary to support research is weak for several reasons. First, an increasing amount of R&D in the United States is being supported by government funding. Second, and more to the point, a greater amount of the extra money charged goes to marketing than to R&D. According to 1999 data, of the top sixteen pharmaceutical companies, only two spent more on R&D than on advertising. Johnson & Johnson, for example, spent approximately 38 percent of its budget on marketing and administration and 9.5 percent on R&D. Merck spent 15.9 percent on marketing and administration and 6.3 percent on R&D. Pfizer spent 39.2 percent on marketing and administration and 17.1 percent on R&D. SmithKline Beecham spent 38.2 percent on marketing and administration and 12.1 percent on R&D. These companies were about in the middle of the pack.[16] According to "Pharmaceutical Drug Companies Killing Middle America Legally While Robbing You Blind," this industry is ranked thirty-fourth among the two hundred U.S. industries with the largest advertising budgets.[17]

The money allocated for advertising is spent in different ways. For example, leaving free samples with practitioners, up to this point in time at least, has been standard practice. My wife is a therapist who recently worked with several psychiatrists in a clinic. Almost every week, she told me, a drug company sales person would show up with free samples as well as an elaborate spread for lunch. The public is bombarded by television commercials, famous for their endnote disclosures warning that the side effects might be dire, that they might include your ears falling off and your nose beginning to glow in the dark. Also, there are direct mailings, posters, and so on, and all of these costs eventually being factored into what the consumer pays.

In countries with a UHS, marketing is not a major expense. At the same time, drugstores and supermarkets in these countries do not provide rows and rows of similar products with different labels competing for your attention. In a pharmacy, you usually have two or three choices, with the druggist suggesting the most appropriate one for your situation.

Finally, another portion of the money earned by pharmaceutical companies is spent on Congressional lobbying. This industry is one of the major contributors to campaigns. At the same time, it reportedly has more lobbyists roaming the halls in Washington than any other. The job of this group is to "encourage" legislators to block bills that might harm their industry's profits. So, through the high prices paid for their medications, consumers are actually supporting efforts of the pharmaceutical industry to block attempts to lower those prices. This is an interesting observation.

Is there an effective way to deal with this issue and to lower pharmaceutical prices? Several alternatives have been suggested. In Canada, for example, the Patent Medicine Prices Review Board establishes and enforces guidelines determining the highest price at which manufacturers can sell brand name drugs. Under these guidelines, the introductory price of a "breakthrough" drug cannot exceed the median price for that drug in other countries. Concerning drugs developed to treat illnesses for which other drugs already exist, their price cannot be higher than that of their competition. Once the introductory price is established, subsequent price increases are determined by changes in the Consumer Price Index.

Another alternative is to open the U.S. market to pharmaceuticals from other countries. The Canadian pricing system just described results in brand name drug prices that are an average of 38 percent lower than prices in the United States, a fact that obviously makes them attractive to U.S. consumers who eagerly buy, usually through the Internet. U.S. pharmaceutical companies, however, have been fighting this practice, supporting legislation that would prohibit it as unfair, which is an extremely interesting stance for an industry that presents itself as a staunch advocate of free enterprise, and a staunch advocate of the right to make as much profit as possible based on the law of supply and demand.

Another approach is to allow government programs, Medicare, Medicaid, etc., to buy drugs in bulk at lower prices, and, better yet, to buy them in bulk from foreign countries, thus ushering in real competition. Unfortunately, the Medicare Prescription Drug Improvement and Modernization Act, passed during the recent Bush administration, prohibited the government from doing this. We must wait and see if the Obama administration is willing and able to overturn the act.

These alternatives again, however, are just band-aids. The only way to truly reduce drug prices is to cap them the way Canada and every other advanced country we have studied does. So long as profit is not regulated, the pharmaceutical companies will continue striving to find ways to increase it, usually at the expense of the consumer. If comprehensive healthcare is to become a right in the United States as it is everywhere else, then the profit motive in pharmaceuticals has to be eliminated, or at least brought under strict control.

Cost of Medical Malpractice Insurance and Malpractice Suits

The term *medical malpractice* refers to professional negligence by act or omission by a healthcare provider in which the care delivered deviates from accepted standards of practice in the medical community and causes injury to the patient. Standards and regulation vary greatly, not only between countries, but between regions within countries. Medical error, which can lead to malpractice suits, remains a serious problem, killing between 44,000 and 98,000 in the United States each year, more than motor vehicle accidents, breast cancer, or AIDS.[18] Some form of malpractice insurance is necessary to serve the interest of patients as well as to protect doctors from financial disaster. The question is: "How best can we make it available?"

Several professional sectors are involved in any malpractice case. The first, obviously, is the healthcare sector: the doctors, nurses, therapists, technicians, nursing home employees, birthing center employees, trauma center employees—those who carry the insurance. The second is the insurance company that issues the policy. The third is the legal profession: the lawyer or law firm handling the case. Then, we have the expert witness or witnesses required for testimony. And, finally, there are the courts.

The relationship between these sectors is hostile. According to healthcare professionals and insurance companies, lawyers do whatever they can to make as much money as possibly. Approximately 54 percent of the reward in every suit won goes for "administrative" costs, most of this being paid to lawyers.[19] At the same time, an increasing number of law firms are refusing to take on such cases due to the high cost of prosecuting them in terms of both money and time.

According to many of the doctors and lawyers we have spoken to, insurance companies practice price gouging whenever they think they can get away with it; the price of premiums continues to rise even when reforms have been put in place in order to hold down the amount awarded by juries.

At the same time, an increasing number of insurance firms are refusing to issue malpractice insurance due to the uncertainty of the market and to the large awards given by juries. Finally, according to many of the insurance company representatives and lawyers we have spoken to, doctors don't want to be held accountable for their mistakes, both avoidable and unavoidable, and don't want to pay the price of raised premiums caused by large awards to victims.

All of these sectors are profit-driven; all can benefit only at the expense of the others. Thus, no common ground can be found. And, ultimately, all can benefit only at the expense of the public being served, the expense of medical errors that have to be lived with, the rising costs of premiums, and the financial burden of law suits eventually being passed on.

Standards, of course, do exist, but, as we have said, they are relatively general. The decisive interpretation is frequently being left up to unsophisticated jury members. Tort reform has been tried and a number of states currently have it in place. But, it has done little to prevent on-going rises in insurance premium rates, with the highest rates currently found in southern Florida where obstetricians and neurosurgeons not employed by the government are required to pay as much as $200,000 per year.[20] Most premiums are lower than that, but paying over $100,000 is no longer a rarity. As a result, physicians are moving to states where the cost is lower or are refusing to perform risky procedures or are deserting their profession entirely. By way of contrast, to show what is possible with a well-designed UHS in place, malpractice insurance in Japan costs between $454 and $491 per year.

Obviously, the malpractice insurance "mess" is extremely complicated. With several competing interests fighting for the profits involved, there seems to be no solution. The most reasonable approach, at this point, might be to take a different perspective. Our model for a UHS that meets the needs of the U.S. population will provide such a perspective.

People Not Doing Their Part and Taking Care of Themselves

This issue brings us back to the system practitioner's belief that no problem stands alone. Of course, a great many U.S. citizens do, indeed, take care of themselves. They find the time to run, work out on gym equipment, watch their diets, don't smoke, and/or don't drink too much. But, then, we have the fact that approximately one-third of the adult U.S. population is obese, meaning that people have too much body fat. Even more alarming is the report that approximately 16.3 percent of our youngsters, ages 2 to 19, are also obese; the trend in both of these populations is headed in the wrong direction.[21]

Also, only a small percentage of us go for semiannual or even annual checkups. We are too busy. We don't want to find out that anything is wrong because we cannot afford it in terms of either money or time.

Another problem is that too many patients, when they are diagnosed with an illness or an injury, do not follow through with their treatment. They don't take their medications conscientiously and don't change their habits as recommended, so that too soon they are back in the doctor's office or in the emergency room.

I do not, however, buy the argument that negligence is the main culprit. Yes, there are a few out there who really don't care about their health, but most people do. For one thing, when we are healthy, we feel better and function better, and thus get more enjoyment out of life.

I believe, instead, that the major culprit is our environment and the demands it places on us. For one thing, it is a lot harder to do the things necessary to stay healthy when you and your spouse are working 50 to 60 hours a week, which is the U.S. average. Due at least partially to these long hours, people in our society spend a great deal of their time feeling tired, and that is not good. When we are tired, we don't really want to cook, so we live on ready-made meals and snacks or go to a restaurant. If we don't have much money, we go to a fast food place.

Besides the long hours, there is the constant pressure to get ahead, so that we are able to afford the latest item used to impress. Such nonending stress takes its toll and makes us more vulnerable physically. And, that stress is emphasized by a marketing culture that surrounds us all day, every day, with commercials, electronic billboards, mailed advertisements, phone surveys, and computer messages that encourage us to eat this or that food because it is really yummy or to buy this or that car or style of clothing because it is the most sought after.

Ultimately, of course, we make our own decisions. That is what democracy is about. That's what our society is about, being able to make our own decisions. However, the science of advertising has become so sophisticated with subliminal messages and such that people are swayed. At the same time, though the amount is growing, we see relatively little advertising that tells us what a healthy life style should be. For example, while we all see plenty of pharmaceutical adds touting the advantages of various drugs, I have yet to see one that says that taking too many medications can easily become a dangerous habit, with an explanation of why this is so, or one that says that getting out for a walk every day will do more for your heart and health than any drug or vitamin on the market.

But, then, where's the profit in that kind of commercial?

Doctors and other healthcare professionals are not equipped to solve the problem of patients not taking care of themselves. It is not their responsibility. They can make suggestions and they can discuss the consequences of not doing so. But, they cannot take the lead in changing a patient's life style because they are just one piece of the puzzle. A comprehensive, highly integrated effort, including the education sector, the world of advertising, the business sector, government, and just about everybody else, needs to be mounted.

Unfortunately, due to the current fragmentation of our society and the conflicting interests we have discussed, such a project would be extremely difficult to organize. But, then, in that the alternative is an increased loss of productivity and of global competitiveness coupled with a continuing rise in the cost of providing healthcare for our citizens, do we have a choice?

The Cost of Education for Healthcare Professionals

The United States is not producing enough doctors to cover our needs. One of the reasons for our overall shortage of doctors is the cost of education. According to the article "Medical School Tuition and Young Physician Indebtedness" (in *Health Affairs: The Policy Journal of the Health Sphere*), in 2005, the average amount of indebtedness for state medical school graduates was $100,000, and for private school graduates, it was $135,000.[22] By the year 2007, both figures had risen, with the latter, at least, to around $150,000.

Both are continuing to climb. According to "Education Debt and Reported Career Plans among Internal Medicine Students" (in *Academia and Clinic: Annals of Internal Medicine)*, an unwillingness to be saddled with such indebtedness is causing many potential young doctors to choose another field.[23] At the same time, a growing number are seeking their training in other countries where it is free or much cheaper. At the same time, the gap in our healthcare system is being filled by newly trained, debt-free doctors immigrating to the United States from foreign countries.

And, of course, doctors are not the only ones who spend years paying off their loans. Nurses, therapists, technicians, administrators, almost everybody ends up bearing a similar burden.

Does this make sense? Does it make sense that too many of our best and brightest do not opt to go into healthcare because they cannot afford the training? While in other countries, medical school graduates are debt-free, or relatively debt-free, in our country, they have to spend years paying off their loans while trying to start a practice.

When taking the on-going stress of such a situation into account, it is not surprising to learn that physicians average 10 to 20 percent more suicides than the general population and 10 to 20 percent more divorces.[24] It is also not surprising to learn that as a result of the limits enforced by healthcare insurance policies, coupled with the cost of malpractice insurance, a lot of doctors, unable to build their income, are giving up and are leaving the field.

Again, does this make sense? Most certainly it does not. If we are going to deliver comprehensive healthcare to our entire population, we need an adequate number of well-trained professionals. In order to produce these professionals, we obviously need to change our approach to their education.

REFERENCES

1. Health Systems Resources (PDF) *World Health Statistics 2008: Global Health Indicators,* World Health Organization, Geneva (2008).
2. *The World Health Report 2000—Health Systems: Improving Performance,* World Health Organization, Geneva 2000.
3. Experts: U.S. Healthcare System Wastes Millions, *The Washington Post,* December 1, 2008.
4. The Amazing, Noncollapsing U.S Health Care System: Is Reform at Hand? Lawrence D. Brown, *New England Journal of Medicine,* 358 (4):325–327, January 24, 2008.

5. Overview of the U.S. Healthcare System, Kao-Ping Chua, American Medical Student Association (AMSA) Jack Rutledge Fellow, February 10, 2006, p. 5.
6. Why Does U.S. Healthcare Cost So Much? Uwe E. Reinhardt, *Economix, Explaining the Science of Everyday Life,* December 12, 2008, p. 2.
7. Chua, Overview of the U.S. Healthcare System, p. 2.
8. Ibid.
9. Experts: U.S. Healthcare System Wastes Millions, *The Washington Post,* December 1, 2008.
10. The Amazing, Noncollapsing U.S Health Care System: Is Reform at Hand? Lawrence D. Brown, *New England Journal of Medicine,* 358 (4):325–327, January 24, 2008.
11. *A Profile of Medicare: Chartbook 1998,* U.S. Health Care Financing Administration, Washington, D.C., May 1998, p. 27.
12. Experts: U.S. Healthcare System Wastes Millions, *The Washington Post,* Monday, December 1, 2008.
13. Healthcare in the United States, *Wikipedia,* p. 4.
14. Basic Questions about Universal Health Care Insurance for All: www.hcforall.org (accessed July 29, 2008).
15. Written Testimony for the Senate Finance Committee Hearing on International Trade and Pharmaceuticals, *Families USA,* April 27, 2004, p. 2.
16. Pharmaceutical Company Expenses: Cost of Sales, Marketing, R&D Compared: www.cptech.org/ip/health/econ/allocation.html (accessed March 16, 2009).
17. Pharmaceutical Drug Companies Killing Middle America Legally While Robbing You Blind: www.betterbodyjournal.com (accessed March 15, 2009).
18. Mythbuster: The Seven Most Important Things to Know about Medical Malpractice, *Center for Justice and Democracy,* February 10, 2004, p. 3.
19. Claims, Errors, and Compensation Payments in Medical Malpractice Litigation, David M. Studdert, Michelle M. Mello, Atul A. Gawande, Tejal K. Gandhi, Allen Kachalia, Catherine Yoon, Ann Louise Puopolo, and Troyen A. Brennan, *New England Journal of Medicine,* 354 (2024–2033): 332–341, May 11, 2006.
20. *The Medical Malpractice Insurance Crisis: Opportunity for State Action,* Princeton, NJ: The Robert Wood Johnson Foundation, July 2002, p. 1.
21. Data on national health and nutrition examination survey 2006. National Institute of Environmental Health Sciences, National Institutes of Health, Bethesda, Maryland, 146 (6): 416–420, September 16, 2008.
22. Medical School Tuition and Young Physicians' Indebtedness, Paul Jolly, *Health Affairs: The Policy Journal of the Health Sphere,* 24, (2): 528, 2005.
23. Educational Debt and Reported Career Plans amongst Internal Medicine Residents, McDonald, F., West, C., Popkave, C., Kolars, J. *Academia and Clinic: Annals of Internal Medicine,* 2008.
24. Physicians Are Not Invincible, *Southern Medical Journal,* 93 (10): 966–972, 2000.

3

Structure and Decision-Making Model in an Idealized Healthcare Network

THE CHALLENGE

The major challenge facing the U.S. healthcare community today is to pull the pieces of our system together into a well-integrated network that provides adequate, cost-effective service to all citizens. At this point, integration of the pieces in our puzzle is, at best, loose. What we have is a conglomerate of private practices, group practices, clinics, for-profit hospitals, not-for-profit hospitals, and government programs funded by multiple sources including federal taxes, state taxes, social security taxes, private insurance companies, and individual out-of-pocket payments.

This is an extremely inefficient, extremely costly approach to organizing an input critical to the advancement of our society. People in many localities (rural, the inner city, etc.) receive inadequate attention, while, in other localities, an abundance of redundancies exist. Some people have excellent insurance. A great many have only partial insurance so that their out-of-pocket costs are extremely high. And, then, approximately 47 million have no insurance at all.

Physicians can sometimes turn away people in need who might have trouble paying. Administrative staff handling reimbursement for providers after the service is delivered must often deal with multiple payers—government, private insurance, and individuals—thus greatly increasing bookkeeping costs. For example, I was recently told by a nurse practitioner working in a clinic that the walls of the office handling reimbursement for her organization were covered from top to bottom by sheets of paper bearing the requirements of different insurance providers.

Other countries ranked higher than the United States by the World Health Organization (WHO) in terms of overall healthcare quality have solved most of these problems. Governments have taken over the placement of healthcare facilities to make sure that every citizen has access to the services offered and to eliminate redundancies. Governments have taken over payment so that everybody can afford the required care. These countries have gone to a one-payer system. The government pays directly or through government-supported insurance funds with a small additional patient co-payment sometimes required.

Many of these more-advanced countries have both a universal healthcare system (UHS) and a private sector in their healthcare system. The government pays for services in the UHS and private sector insurance companies cover the cost of services in the private sector. Only in Italy can doctors work in both the UHS and private sectors.[1] In Japan, while there is private insurance, there are no private sector physicians. Therefore, people holding private insurance must seek help from the same professionals who people without private insurance use, possibly paying more than is required of UHS patients, and possibly hoping for a higher quality of care.

We shall begin our effort to design an ideal structure for the U.S. healthcare system by focusing on the organization of the facility network and on the management system put into place to effectively integrate this network. We shall discuss the role of decision-making boards of directors established at the federal, state, regional, and local levels; the administration hierarchy, the integration of regional research/teaching/medical hospitals, general hospitals, specialized clinics, community health centers and their satellites, and nursing homes. We shall also design into our model a private sector including private practices and private hospitals that are paid for with private sector healthcare insurance.

But, first, as we have said, we need to explore what other countries have come up with in order to learn from their efforts, their successes, and their mistakes.

France

France's universal healthcare system was ranked No. 1 by the 2000 WHO report. Private insurance can be bought in France as well. A majority of

French citizens buy it so that they can use both systems. In the French model, the public and private sectors generally cooperate rather than compete. This is one of the system's strengths and allows citizens to avoid the waiting lists for surgeries associated with socialized medicine in other countries and to avoid the need for preauthorization. Indeed, private medical care in France is particularly active in this area, treating more than 50 percent of overall surgeries and more than 60 percent of cancer cases.[2]

The law guarantees patients the right to choose their practitioner in the French system. At the other end of the spectrum, the law also guarantees physicians control over medical decision making, which is a major problem in the United States with insurance companies forcing their will.

The French system centers on hospitals. The hospital network includes public hospitals, with the larger, teaching ones usually found in major cities; private for-profit hospitals; and private not-for-profit hospitals. The public hospital system is the largest, which controls 65 percent of the country's available beds.

In the public sector, three levels of hospitals exist. *General hospitals* spread throughout the country offer the widest range of services including acute care (medicine, surgery, and obstetrics), follow-up care, rehabilitation, psychiatry, and long-term care. *Regional hospitals* are more specialized and more comprehensive in their areas of expertise. Usually they are teaching hospitals linked with universities. *Local hospitals* offer general services, but are not used for surgery or childbirth.

Physicians and other healthcare professionals generally work from their own practices. Treatment not requiring hospitalization is typically provided by these practices. Health centers exist, but are used as much in France as they are in other countries.[3]

To relieve pressure on hospitals, a Hospitalization at Home system has been in place for over forty years. Nurses and other professionals provide continuous home care for patients suffering chronic or terminal illnesses. The efforts of these people are coordinated and facilitated by doctors available for consultation at any time over the telephone.

The French use a system similar to our 911 emergency number to move home patients and new patients rapidly when immediate care is necessary to the most appropriate specialized facility, thus cutting down on visits to hospital emergency rooms. France is also a leader in the development and use of Smart Card technology, the computerized Smart Card carrying a patient's medical background. This is a new concept that will be discussed in more detail in the chapter on information technology.

Key Features of the French System

1. Physicians generally work out of their own practices rather than community health centers.
2. Beyond primary care physicians, hospitals are the major players: *local hospitals* provide general care but no surgery, *regional hospitals* provide more specialized care, and *general hospitals* provide the widest range of overall care.
3. The UHS- and private insurance-funded sectors coordinate efforts rather than competing. Physicians can work in only one sector.
4. Emphasis is placed on home care, with physicians and other professionals making home visits.
5. A 911-type system is used to ensure that patients in need are sent to the most appropriate facility.
6. All French citizens carry Smart Cards that are computerized and contain their medical background.

Italy

Italy, ranked second by the 2000 WHO report, like most other European nations has made decentralization its priority. The country's three-tiered system for administering healthcare has the Federal Ministry of Health at the top, twenty-one regional administrative units in the middle, and approximately two hundred Local Health Agencies plus one hundred hospitals at the bottom.[4]

Local health agencies and hospitals in Italy are totally responsible for meeting the healthcare needs of the population served. All citizens carry a national health card that ensures treatment in any part of the country. Citizens must, by law, enroll with a general practitioner (GP) or pediatrician, but can pick their own doctor, who refers them to specialists when needed. Emergency appointments are scheduled within forty-eight hours.

A unique feature of the Italian approach is the degree of cooperation that exists between local health agencies. A reimbursement system exists that allows units to cover expenses for treating each other's clients. This might be used when an overload occurs and clients need to be sent elsewhere, when specialized care is required, or when somebody breaks a leg while away from home.

Also, over 3,000 Guardia Medica stations are spread throughout the country with a physician on call at each site twenty-four hours a day.[5] As has been said, physicians in Italy are allowed to treat patients paying through the UHS as well as those paying with supplementary private insurance.

Each region in Italy has been given the authority to levy its own taxes for healthcare in order to complement what is received from the central government. The central government can also help regions suffering from a deficit through the National Solidarity Fund. This fund transfers, at the federal level, monies from regions showing a surplus in their budget to those having problems meeting expenses. Because no profit motive and no competition exists, because the network's objective is to provide high-quality healthcare for all citizens, such transfers of funds are not usually a problem.

Key Features of the Italian System

1. All hospitals, as well as local health agencies, are located and administered at the local level. None are administered at any level above (regional, national).
2. All citizens carry a National Health Card that allows them to be treated anywhere in the country.
3. Citizens must, by law, enroll with a GP or pediatrician, but can pick their own doctor.
4. Taxes to support the UHS are raised both at the federal and regional level.
5. The central government can transfer funds from regions showing a surplus to those experiencing deficits through its National Solidarity Fund.
6. Guardia Medica stations provide around-the-clock emergency services.
7. Physicians can treat both UHS patients and those carrying private insurance.

Sweden

The Swedish healthcare system, ranked twenty-third by the WHO, is controlled at the federal level by the National Board of Health and Welfare whose mission is *to ensure the fundamental human right of all citizens to obtain adequate and equitable healthcare.* Emphasis at this point in the Swedish system is on improving prevention services and on cutting costs. The National Board distributes tax-based funds to six regions that coincide with the political regions in which the country is divided. These regions are then responsible for the further dispersion of funds and for formulating regional policy. The National Board, however, retains ultimate authority and can overrule regional decisions, though it rarely does.

The National Board also is responsible for supporting the activities of a Committee of Inquiry formed to study social, economic, immigration, and work-related trends that might call for changes in the system or changes in the allocation of funds or changes in the amount of responsibility exercised by the regions.[6]

Concerning the provision of services, the Swedish healthcare system includes four levels. Local health centers are situated in individual communities and provide primary care and are staffed by general practitioners, nurses, auxiliary nurses, midwives, physiotherapists, occupational therapists, social workers, and psychologists. Special treatment programs focused on prevention are offered by the centers. They include maternity clinics and child clinics where periodic examinations and inoculations are received.

Patients are free to pick their physician and are free to go to a different center if they wish. Appointments have to be scheduled by the staff within eight days of a patient request. If this is not possible, the patient can ask that an appointment be made at another center. The cost for transportation to all medical facilities is reimbursed.

The Swedish government provides a user-friendly *Guide to Healthcare* available to everybody—healthcare personnel and patients—that explains ailments and symptoms. Local health centers also offer a twenty-four-hour helpline service manned by experienced nurses who answer health-related questions and make treatment recommendations, as well as a twenty-four-hour emergency line service, a twenty-four-hour pharmaceutical telephone information service, and a twenty-four-hour telephone poison information center service.

At the county level, hospitals provide care in a number of specialized areas on both an inpatient and an outpatient basis. Hospitals at the district level also treat basic illnesses and injuries, though the range treated is broader than that found at the county level. Patients can be sent here from local centers without first going through the county level.

Ten major teaching hospitals are found at the regional level. A majority of the surgery is done in these. The most sophisticated technology is found here. Patients can be referred directly from local health centers without first going through the county and district levels. Patients can also make an appointment themselves and frequently do, expecting better treatment at this level.

Approximately 75 percent of the entire Swedish healthcare budget is spent on the hospital sector, most at the upper levels. The federal Committee of Inquiry is currently looking for ways to make lower level services more attractive. Regional governments manage all hospitals in the network. In many cases, however, they have been turned over to local boards of trustees who control daily operations and run them as not-for-profit organizations. As a result, Sweden has a combination of public sector ownership and private sector operation.

Tax-based revenues are distributed by the National Board of Health and Welfare to the six regions based on projected need. The regional governments then allocate them to district and county levels. Individual counties are divided into medical areas that have governing boards. The county council, an elected body responsible for all public services, argues its yearly healthcare budget requirement at the regional level. Funds allocated to each county are then divided among the medical area boards and distributed to hospitals and the local health centers.

All healthcare employees are salaried, with pay levels being set by county councils. Approximately 75 percent of facility expenses are covered by the monies received from the regional level. Approximately 15 percent are covered by local taxes levied by the council. The remainder is covered by a patient co-payment, which normally ranges from 10 to 15 percent based on the judgment of the council and on the financial status of the facility.

County councils are not expected to allow deficits. They have the power to manipulate local taxes as well as the amount that patients co-pay in order to avoid a deficit. If one does occur, the council has two years to erase it. A safeguard is a federal mandate that local authorities must have periodic audits. The government can also provide "equalization grants" to help ease deficits.

One more responsibility of county councils is the formation of a Patients' Committee for Complaints, a group responsible for listening to and trying to help resolve patient issues.

Key Features of the Swedish System

1. The system is controlled by a National Board of Health and Welfare whose mission is to ensure the fundamental human right of all citizens to obtain adequate and equitable healthcare.
2. A Committee of Inquiry at the national level studies social, economic, immigration, and work-related trends that might necessitate changes in the system.
3 Four levels of facilities exist: local health centers, county level hospitals (more specialized), district level hospitals, and regional teaching hospitals (surgery).
4. Local health centers are staffed by general practitioners, nurses, auxiliary nurses, midwives, physiotherapists, occupational therapists, social workers, and psychologists.
5. Citizens are free to pick their own local health center and their own physician.
6. A twenty-four-hour emergency "help line" is available to patients.
7. A patients Committee for Complaints exists at the county level.

Finland

Primary healthcare in Finland is provided by municipal health centers. A municipality may run its own center if demand is great enough or may run one in conjunction with other municipalities. These centers offer more than similar centers in other countries. The services provided include preventative education and care, outpatient care, inpatient care, dental care, maternity care, child healthcare, care for the elderly, family planning, physiotherapy, and occupational healthcare. The centers are allowed to establish satellites when the need arises. Each citizen or family picks a primary doctor at the center who then refers patients to specialists.

Finland has been divided into twenty hospital districts, each including several municipalities, each containing at least one central hospital as well as satellite hospitals. The level of care at central hospitals is more sophisticated, so that satellite hospitals can refer patients. Of the central hospitals, five are university hospitals offering the highest level of specialized care. All central and satellite hospitals from all districts can refer patients to these facilities.

Finland has gone perhaps the farthest in terms of decentralizing authority and responsibility. In 1990, the Finnish central government financed roughly

35.6 percent of national healthcare costs, while in the year 2000 it financed only 18 percent. In 1990, the municipalities, which are similar to our counties, financed 34.7 percent, while in 2000 they were responsible for 42 percent.[7]

Key Features of the Finnish System

1. Finland has been divided into twenty hospital districts, each including at least one central hospital with the most sophisticated technology and several satellite hospitals.
2. Of the central hospitals, five are university hospitals offering the highest level of care.
3. Communities are served by municipal health centers that provide an unusually wide range of services and are allowed to create satellites.
4. The municipalities rather than the central government provide most of the funding, more than 50 percent at this point, while the government provides less than 20 percent.

European Union

As an added note of interest, Europeans are apparently thinking systemically as well in their efforts to improve healthcare. A project to develop a "seamless system" is underway not only in individual countries, but in the European Union as a whole. Currently, member country citizens can receive treatment in other member countries, but must fill out forms in order to do so. However, a European Health Insurance Card similar to the French Smart Card is being developed that will be carried by everybody and will tie into the European Union universal information systems also being developed, thus eliminating the paperwork.

Japan

The Japanese healthcare system is different in several ways from those previously described. Like the others, it is government funded and regulated. No private sector exists. Insurance is bought from several sources, all of which are government regulated. The major difference has to do with the delivery system. Japan does not have general practitioners. All physicians are specialized. As a result, there is no primary physician to go to initially. The patient is sent on to a specialist if need be. Also, there are no community health centers offering a variety of services. What exist in Japanese cities are specialized clinics competing for customers, and then the hospital system. Only in rural areas, due to a relative shortage of physicians, do they offer a variety of services.

As a result of this arrangement, relatively little attention is paid to preventative medicine. If a person catches a cold, he or she goes to an internal medicine clinic for treatment, but only after the cold is contracted. Periodic checkups are not possible without going to a variety of clinics. Preventative measures are encouraged mainly by the government. For example, the government recently sent information to overweight people describing the damage this condition can cause and recommending ways to deal with it. Also, the government has tried to address the problem of cigarette smoking, which is so prevalent in the country, especially among young men. But one-on-one examinations and follow-up on the general state of a patient's health are extremely rare due to the lack of primary physicians and community centers focused on health maintenance.

Key Features of the Japanese System

1. It is government funded; insurance is bought from public sector sources. There is no private sector practice. There are no private sector insurance companies.
2. There are no general practitioners; all physicians are specialized. Only in rural areas do physicians offer a range of services.
3. There are no community healthcare centers, only clinics offering specialized service.
4. Prevention is not a priority. Periodic physical examinations are not encouraged.
5. The government takes the lead in preventative education.

AN IDEALIZED STRUCTURE FOR A U.S. UHS

Feeding off concepts and designs found in other countries, we will now attempt to remodel the current U.S. healthcare establishment into a joint public sector (UHS)/private sector system that includes some existing pieces and concepts, but eliminates or radically changes others, and that also add new ones. Our model will include a hierarchy of governing boards, a hierarchy of administrative departments, and a three-tiered hierarchy of delivery facilities.

In terms of UHS governance, there will be:

1. A National UHS Board of Directors
2. UHS boards of directors for six national regions
3. State UHS boards of directors
4. Local UHS network boards of directors

In terms of UHS administration, there will be:

1. A national Department of Healthcare Administration
2. State Departments of Healthcare Administration including a State Ethics Panel
3. Local Departments of Healthcare Administration including a local patient committee for complaints similar to that found in Sweden.

In terms of UHS service delivery, there will be:

1. Research/teaching/medical hospitals
2. General hospitals
3. Specialized clinics
4. Community health centers
5. Community healthcare center satellites
6. Nursing homes

In terms of service delivery in the private sector, there will be:

1. Private, for-profit hospitals
2. Private nursing homes
3. Private practices

UHS Governance System

The National UHS Board of Directors

National headquarters for the UHS will be under the auspices of the Department of Health and Human Services (DHHS) in Washington, D.C.

Currently, the executive director of DHHS is appointed by the president of the United States and serves on the president's cabinet. This arrangement will be modified so that the executive director continues to be a presidential nominee, though his or her appointment will be subject to the initial and continuing approval of a newly formed, nonpolitical National UHS Board of Directors. An appointment can be blocked by a majority vote of the board. Also, based on performance, the board can vote to remove that person from the position and allow the president to appoint a new secretary. The executive director will function as the channel between the National UHS Board of Directors and the federal government. While the government decides the UHS budget, as it does in the other countries studied, it cannot use this leverage to dictate UHS policy.

The purpose of the National UHS Board of Directors will be:

- To set national healthcare policy
- To head on-going national level planning
- To help integrate efforts of the regional UHS boards of directors
- To monitor performance at the regional level
- To facilitate healthcare education and system improvement efforts at the national level
- To decide the amount of tax-based funds to be distributed to each region for healthcare professional salaries, facility improvements, and equipment updates
- To set base salary levels for UHS teams and employees
- To decide on a schedule of fees for services delivered by the UHS
- To decide the size of the individual citizen's healthcare allowance
- To release emergency funds to the regions

The amount of tax-based funds distributed to each region will depend, as in Norway as described in Chapter 4, on the characteristics of that region's population and will change as those characteristics change. In terms of the individual citizen's healthcare allowance, the only variant will be age, with people in each age group receiving the same amount yearly. The involved money will never actually change hands. The allowance will be allotted electronically, and payments will be made from it electronically.

The National UHS Board of Directors will also be responsible for assessing and promoting Expert Panel reports that are currently generated on an ongoing basis by the National Institutes of Health (NIH) and the Agency for Healthcare Research and Quality (AHRQ). These expert panel reports will focus on two things. The first, as in Sweden, will be Committee of Inquiry-type information concerning social, economic, immigration, and work-related trends that might call for changes in the UHS. The second thing focused on will be best practices derived from "evidence-based medicine," a concept currently being discussed widely in the literature. Decisions will be driven by clinical trial datasets gained from a universal information system that will be part of the UHS.

Expert panels will convene at regular intervals (e.g., every three years) and will be comprised of nationally recognized healthcare researchers and clinicians representing a broad mix of healthcare disciplines and residing in geographically diverse regions of the country. These experts will evaluate research findings and decide through consensus both necessary changes in UHS policy and the best practices clinicians should follow in order to assure quality outcomes while containing cost. The National UHS Board of Directors will be responsible for ensuring that these evidence-based medicine guidelines are implemented. The board will also be responsible for benchmarking data gained from the UHS information system as a vehicle for measuring the success of implementation.

The nonpolitical National UHS Board of Directors will seat a range of people including representatives from:

- Regions: One representative from each of the six regional UHS boards of directors selected by the members of that board.
- Federal government: This will be necessary because the UHS's primary funding source will be taxes. Three people—one Democrat, one Republican, one Independent—will be appointed by the U.S. Senate for a four-year renewable term that runs parallel to that of the U.S. president.
- The National Department of Healthcare Administration: The executive director of UHS administration, the operations officer, and the financial officer will be board members.

Regional UHS Boards of Directors

The United States, as we have said, will be divided into six regions for the purpose of delivering healthcare. Representatives appointed by the governors of the states in each region will sit on the Regional UHS Board of Directors. These representatives will be nominated by members of the state UHS boards of directors and recommended to the governor. Responsibilities of the Regional UHS Board of Director's will include:

- To set regional policy
- To facilitate region-level planning based on plans received from the national level
- To help integrate efforts of the state UHS boards of directors
- To decide how much money each UHS State Department of Healthcare Administration should receive for employee salaries, facility improvements, and equipment updates
- To monitor performance at the state level
- To facilitate education and system improvement efforts at the state level
- To release emergency funds to the state level when necessary, say, when a natural disaster such as a hurricane occurs

Because no administrative function will exist at this level, no administrators will be members of the board. Decisions made by regional UHS boards of directors can be overridden only by the National UHS Board of Directors.

State UHS Boards of Directors

A representative from each of the local UHS network boards of directors will sit on the State Board of Directors. Because an administrative function will exist at this level, the executive director, operations officer, and financial officer of the State Department of Healthcare Administration will also sit on the board. This group's responsibilities will include:

- To set statewide policy
- To head the on-going state level planning effort based on plans received from the regional level
- To decide how much federal tax-based money each local network should receive for salaries, facility improvements, equipment updates, etc.

- To set the amount of state healthcare taxes required to supplement the federal funds received if a need is determined
- To help integrate the work of research/teaching/medical hospitals, general hospitals, specialized clinics, nursing homes, and community health centers in the state's networks
- To monitor the performance of these organizations
- To facilitate education and system improvement efforts begun by the involved organizations
- To release emergency funds to the local level when necessary
- To create a State Ethics Board to review and pass judgment on cases sent up from local networks

Local UHS Boards of Directors

Each state will be divided into local networks based on population. Each local network will center on a research/teaching/medical hospital. Each local network will be governed by a Local UHS Board of Directors. The board's members will include four UHS professions with different backgrounds. Because an administrative function will exist at the local level, the board will also include the director, operations officer, and financial officer of the local Department of Healthcare Administration. Finally, the Local UHS Board of Directors will include representatives from the Facility Advisory Committees (discussed later) in the area. The local board's responsibilities will include:

- To set local policy
- To head the on-going local planning effort based on plans received from the state level
- To decide how funds received from the state administrative level for salaries, facility improvements, and equipment upgrades should be divided among network operations
- To help integrate the work of facilities in the local network
- To monitor the performance of these organizations
- To facilitate education and system improvement efforts begun by the involved organizations

An additional responsibility of the local board will be to establish a Patient Issue Panel similar to the Patients' Committee for Complaints found in Sweden composed of healthcare network staff and community representatives. When a legal or ethical issue is brought to the panel's attention, say, a surgeon mistakenly cuts off the wrong leg due to a lack of appropriate information, or a healthcare facility staff member makes sexual advances toward a patient during an examination, and the panel feels unqualified to deal with it, the issue may be referred to the State Ethics Board, which has been assembled by and reports to the State UHS Department of Administration.

UHS Administration System

The National UHS Department of Healthcare Administration

The system administering the UHS will have three levels: national, state, and local. The personnel structure at both the national level and the state level will include an executive director, an operations officer, and a financial officer. Personnel found in local UHS Departments of Healthcare Administration will include a medical director with administrative skills as well as an understanding of local healthcare issues, a financial officer, a director of social work, a director of information systems, a director of healthcare specialists, a director of staff training, and a director of on-going patient education.

The responsibilities of the National UHS Department of Healthcare Administration will include:

- To oversee administrative unit efforts at the state level
- To allocate tax-based funds approved by the National UHS Board of Directors for employee salaries, facility improvements, and equipment updates to state Departments of Healthcare Administration
- To promote the incorporation of evidence-based medicine (EBM) into practices within each state
- To help administrative departments at the state level learn from each other, to ensuring that data on healthcare outcomes and cost is shared by states so they can benchmark best practices
- To integrate state efforts when beneficial
- To help hold down administrative costs
- To organize and oversee operation of the six regional Universal Information System (UIS) hubs that tie the UIS together nationally, into which the local network data banks feed

State UHS Departments of Healthcare Administration

The responsibilities of the State UHS Department of Healthcare Administration will include:

- To oversee local network efforts within that state and to troubleshoot administrative problems
- To allocate tax-based funds received from the Federal Department of Healthcare Administration to local Departments of Healthcare Administration for salaries, facility improvement, and equipment upgrades within their networks
- To allocate funds raised through a state tax (if necessary) for healthcare to local Departments of Healthcare Administration
- To maintain service delivery records and records of payments received from patient allowances to be used when the State UHS Board of Directors argues yearly at the regional level for funding
- To maintain and upgrade information technology statewide
- To monitor the quality of care provided statewide
- To take the lead in planning and integrating the statewide Health Education Program with input from hospitals, specialized clinics, and community centers as well as from state and local boards of directors
- To make sure new ideas concerning both treatment and education are disseminated throughout the state network and are passed up to the National Department of Healthcare Administration for further dissemination
- To form a State Ethics Panel that deals with complaints including legal and ethical concerns passed up from local network Patient Issue Panels
- To oversee the state UHS minibus transportation system and trouble-shoot it

Local UHS Departments of Healthcare Administration

The responsibilities of the Local UHS Department of Healthcare Administration will include:

- To oversee administration of the local network's research/teaching/medical hospital, of the network's general hospitals, specialized clinics, nursing homes, and community health centers, and to troubleshoot

- To allocate funds received from the State Department of Healthcare Administration for salaries, facility improvements, and equipment updates
- To house the data bank for the local UIS that feeds into one of the six integrated regional "hub" data banks
- To troubleshoot UIS issues for the network research/teaching/ medical hospital; for general hospitals, specialized clinics, nursing homes, and community health centers
- To schedule the movement of specialists between network facilities
- To facilitate the movement of patients between network facilities when necessary
- To provide on-going training for the staff of all facilities
- To modify the state sponsored patient health education program to meet local network needs
- To support education efforts mounted by individual units
- To manage the minibus transportation system

UHS Service Delivery

In our discussion of UHS service delivery, we will start at the bottom of the ladder this time instead of the top.

Community Health Centers

At least one health center will be placed in every community of any size. In rural areas one center may serve several communities, as in Finland. Daily staff will include a medical director, a director of finance, at least one family practice physician, physician's assistants, nurses, social workers, healthcare educators who travel through the community dispensing information, and a pharmacist, The responsibilities of the social worker in this scenario will include advocating for a patient's rights and helping to discover and address issues affecting recovery that lie outside the healthcare system. Social workers will be expected to familiarize themselves with the patient's background and family as well as that person's home and work environment.

As in Sweden and Italy, each family will have one primary care giver. Families, including a member or members with complex medical conditions, will usually be allowed to pick a physician as their care-giver. Families with no member "at risk" will choose between available nurse practitioners and physician assistants. If the family's situation changes, it can be reassigned so that a different level of care might be received. An attending nurse practitioner or physician's assistant can also refer a patient to a physician.

"Visiting" staff will move through the local network spending time at each facility. Their visits will be scheduled by the local UHS Department of Healthcare Administration. Visiting staff will include nutritionists/dieticians, physiologists, physiotherapists, occupational therapists, speech therapists, and psychologists. Their responsibilities will include the authority to recommend that patients be sent to specialty clinics or that they be admitted to a general hospital or to the research/teaching/medical hospital for more intensive care.

Each Community Health Center will be supported by a volunteer advisory group composed of community members. The center medical director will sit with this group along with the director of finance. One of the strengths of the advisory group set-up is that it allows individual centers to adapt more easily to local conditions and local demands.

Community health centers will be equipped with a lab as well as with x-ray, pharmaceutical, and other routine equipment. A small pharmacy will be part of the operation so patients can pick up their medications immediately. Prescriptions will be transmitted electronically from the physician to the druggist, an automatic check being made against the patient's records. This procedure will facilitate the process and help eliminate abuse. The community health centers will have beds, but only for emergencies. Patients needing a bed and on-going attention will be transported to a specialized clinic or a hospital as quickly as possible. As in Italy, service will be available twenty-fours hours a day. A skeleton staff will remain at the center at night, but will have telephone access to other staff on an as-needed basis. Each center will house several minivans used to transport patients.

When a center serves a large geographic area, usually in a rural setting, or when the population served has trouble reaching the center for reasons, such as poverty or old age, center satellites can be established. In all satellite offices, the team will be built around a nurse practitioner. The team will include a registered nurse, a social worker, and other personnel considered necessary. For example, in a poor neighborhood, a nutritionist might be a part of the team. In a retirement home, a physiotherapist might be a part of the team. Other specialists, such as psychologists, can visit on a rotating or an as-needed basis. When a patient's problem cannot be dealt with at the satellite, that person will be transported to the appropriate community health center, specialized clinic, or hospital. The satellites will only be open from 8 a.m. to 8 p.m.

Again, each satellite will be supported by a volunteer advisory group seating representatives of the neighborhood served.

A satellite office will be set up in each public school in the local network. The most important service provided will be the periodic checkup. Like all other recipients of the UHS allowance, introduced in Chapter 4, students will be required to have two checkups a year. All students will be screened on an on-going basis so that diseases and disabilities can be detected early.

Another service provided through school satellites will be the delivery of comprehensive educational programs promoting good healthcare habits. A third service provided will be the monitoring of health-related school activities. Based on what is seen, recommendations will be made to the school board. An example of this last service would be to survey the types of food available to students in the cafeteria, to survey the types available from vending machines, and to make recommendations based on nutritional value.

If the school board does not take advantage of the advice offered, the issue can be referred to the Local UHS Board of Directors who can contact the local Department of Education.

School satellite staff will treat minor ailments onsite. Staff will also be able to send students to community health centers, specialized clinics, or hospitals. Doctors, as well as other specialists, will be on call for emergencies. Each program will also have access to emergency transportation on an as-needed basis. School satellites will be on the schedules of the "visiting" specialists who are part of that local network's system.

All services delivered at the school facility will be considered preventative and, therefore, will be free. Payment for services rendered when a student is sent to a community health center, a specialized clinic, or a hospital will be deducted from that individual's healthcare allowance. The school satellite program will help reach children whose parents neglect their health or whose parents are trying to make money from the healthcare allowance by depriving them of necessary attention. Parents who prefer that their child use a community health center physician or a private physician when a checkup is due must present documented evidence to the school satellite staff that the required service has been delivered elsewhere.

Because an advisory group for each public school already exists (the PTA), it is not necessary to form a separate one for the satellite healthcare program. However, a Health Advisory Subcommittee should be made part of the PTA structure. Membership of the subcommittee will include the nurse practitioner or physician's assistant heading the school satellite, a representative from the local community health center, and parents. Representatives from the local UHS Department of Healthcare Administration and the Local UHS Board of Directors will be "on call" if input is needed.

The Health Advisory Subcommittee will report to the PTA not only on school program concerns, but will also provide updates on healthcare issues in the district and state. For example, the subcommittee will report on new viruses that have surfaced and on the availability of immunizations for students. It will also report on relevant healthcare policy changes that have occurred at the state level.

Satellite offices will be established at UHS-funded nursing homes, the staff again centering around a nurse practitioner or physician's assistant. Some of the satellite offices of the network's community health centers will be on wheels. Well-equipped vans will take the place of China's "barefoot doctors," who were those practicing medicine in rural areas who never formally attended school. They learned their trade as apprentices to doctors who had been in practice for many years and had learned their skills the same way. These "barefoot doctors," continuing a centuries-old Chinese tradition, will travel to isolated areas. The vans can also help out on-sight in emergencies—fires, floods, train wrecks, etc. They can assist when large numbers of people need to be treated or inoculated.

An easily accessible online information channel similar to Sweden's *Guide to Healthcare* will be established where anybody—healthcare providers or patients—can learn about various ailments, about various symptoms, and what they might indicate.

Both community health centers and their satellites will be tied into telephone helplines for emergencies, pharmaceutical information, and poison information. The system will again be similar to that found in the Sweden, providing answers to treatment questions and allowing staff to deal quickly with situations requiring a greater degree of expertise or more sophisticated technology.

Patients will have access to a separate channel of the helpline from their homes or other locations in order to receive preventative advice and treatment advice for minor maladies—colds, scrapes and bruises, etc.—as well as advice for emergencies when something has to be done immediately—choking, poisoning, etc.

Telemedicine will be made available by local community health centers. This service will be further discussed in Chapter 5, which presents our design for the UHS information system.

In the private sector, individual and group practices that take only private insurance will set up wherever they wish. A way the private sector can complement the UHS is by setting up its own satellites to offer convenient, relatively inexpensive service in locations that fills gaps in the UHS network. An example would be the healthcare currently offered by Walmart® stores. The Walmart corporation leases space to private clinics. People simply walk into a Walmart clinic and pay a flat fee of around $45 per visit; first come, first serve. If given a prescription, they can fill it at the in-store pharmacy, often paying as little as $4. Such private sector satellites will allow people greater access. Obviously, if the staff in these satellites run into something they are not prepared to deal with, they can refer the individual to a private physician or hospital. Staff can also refer that person to a UHS community health center, a UHS clinic, or a UHS hospital.[8]

Specialized Clinics

In the countries we have studied thus far, with the exception of Japan, specialized clinics play little, if any role. Most have private practices or community centers at the local level, then either general or more specialized hospitals that physicians and centers refer patients to. France, however, does have some clinics that focus on issues including vision, AIDS, and dentistry.

After Japan, the United States has done the most with this concept. The yellow pages of our telephone books contain a relatively large section on clinics that focus on just about every condition including sports injuries, childhood health (obstetrics), orthopedics (bones and joints), nephrology (kidneys), ophthalmology (eyes), dermatology (skin), mental health, dentistry, heart, and peripheral vascular surgery. Clinics are so popular in the United States at least partially because, in our private insurance-based healthcare system, specialists make more money than GPs. As a result of this incentive, 60 percent of our medical students have, at least in the recent past, chosen to specialize.

In the UHS being designed, specialized clinics will continue to play a role. Their location will be based on population statistics gained from the

UIS that will be part of the UHS. Services offered at each clinic will also be determined through analysis of UIS information in conjunction with input from the Local UHS Board of Directors, the medical directors of local community health centers, and from center advisory committees. Clinic staff will include a medical director, doctors with appropriate skills, physician's assistants, nurses, and social workers.

Patients can be sent from one specialized clinic to another that offers the same specialty when the workload grows too heavy. Also, in special cases, when special skills are needed, staff can be temporarily borrowed from other clinics. Specialized clinics will have beds. Some patients will stay for extended periods of time. Terminal cancer patients will stay in a clinic that specializes in cancer treatment; AIDS victims will stay in a clinic that focuses on AIDS treatment. Hospitals, as well as community health centers, will refer patients requiring extended or more intensive treatment and care to clinics.

Only walk-out, same-day surgery where the patient is not anesthetized will be performed at the specialized clinics. To enter a clinic, except in an emergency, the patient will need a release signed by their primary care giver at the community health center

Private sector specialized clinics dependent on private insurance will exist as well. As in France, specialists must choose between the public and private sectors. They will not be allowed to work at a clinic in both.

General Hospitals

Each local network of community health centers and specialized clinics will contain at least one general hospital, where the number, size, and location of these hospitals is based on population statistics. The general hospitals will offer a broad range of services. Again, they will be allowed to refer patients to other general hospitals when full and to share staff. Top-level technology will be found at these general hospitals and state-of-the-art emergency rooms will be found here. Specialists affiliated with local clinics will be allowed to perform more complex surgery that requires anesthesia. In order to be admitted to a general hospital, except in an emergency, patients will need a release signed by their primary care giver at the community health center or from a physician at the specialized clinic their primary caregiver sent them to.

Each general hospital will have an advisory committee including representatives from all the community health centers served, a representative from the local UHS Board of Directors, a representative from the local UHS Department of Administration, the hospital executive director, the medical director, the director of finance, and the director of operations.

There will also be private for-profit and not-for-profit hospitals in the area covered by the UHS network that people with private insurance can choose to use.

Regional Research, Teaching/Medical Hospitals

One research/teaching/medical hospital will be the hub of at least one network of community health centers, their satellites, specialized clinics, and general hospitals. It will be the largest facility in the network and house the most beds. It will have strong ties with the academic community and will be used as a teaching arena by medical schools in the area. Surgery of the most complex nature will be performed here (open heart, brain, etc.). Patients with unusual illnesses and those needing isolation will be treated here. To enter, patients will need a referral signed by a general hospital physician, a specialized clinic physician, or their primary caregiver at the community health center.

The research/teaching/medical hospital can also be used to handle overflow if the general hospitals and specialized clinics served are full. The emergency room at this hospital will function as a harbor of last resort, all emergencies being sent initially to a general hospital.

The research/teaching/medical hospital will be advised by a committee seating representatives of the general hospitals, specialized clinics, and community health centers served. A representative of the local UHS Board of Directors and a representative of the local UHS Department of Administration will also sit on it, as well as the hospital executive director, the medical director, the director of finances, and the director of operations.

Implementation

A comprehensive plan for implementing the national UHS will first need to be developed. The location and size of each network in each state will be defined. This effort will be conducted at the state level, controlled by the state boards of directors. After the plan is completed, local boards of directors will be formed to fit the network model.

Obviously, implementation will be impossible to do all at once. After the necessary boards of directors and Departments of Healthcare Administration have been formed at all levels, money will be allocated by the National Board of Directors directly to the state Departments of Healthcare Administration to establish one pilot network in each state. This pilot will be used as a model by the other networks when they receive funding.

Compliance to systems specifications defined in the national UHS plan will be monitored by the State Board of Directors. If the specifications are not met, the state boards can recommend a withdrawal or withholding of funds until they are. The Regional Boards of Directors will provide a higher level of oversight and a court of appeals if the State Department of Administration does not agree with the State Board of Directors' decision. The Regional Boards can reverse state board decisions or agree to withhold federal funds.

REFERENCES

1. The Italian Healthcare System: W.H.O. Ranking versus Public Perception, V. Maio, and L. Manzoli, *P&T*, 27 (6): 301–308, 2002.
2. France's Model Healthcare System, Paul V. Dutton, *The Boston Globe*, August 11, 2007, A11.
3. The French Healthcare System: A Brief Overview, *CREDES*, October 2001.
4. The Italian Healthcare System, 2002.
5. The Italian National Health System: www.globalcitizenship.at/workspace/att/file98984926.doc (accessed February 10, 2009).
6. Local Government in Sweden, Organization, Activities and Finance, *The Ministry of Finance:* http://www.finans.regeringen.se (accessed December 5, 2004).
7. *The Role of Decentralization of European Health Care Systems*, V. Bankauskaite, R.B. Saltman, and K. Vrangbaek, Report to IPPR, European Observatory of Health Systems and Policies and Department of Political Science, University of Copenhagen, February 2004.
8. Private Sector Healthcare Leads the Way, Chris Brown, *Mises Daily*, December 3, 2008: http://mises.org/story/3233 (accessed January 12, 2009).

4

Network Financial Model

THE CHALLENGE

Our healthcare system obviously needs fixing. It is not cost effective when compared to that of other developed countries, and it does not provide the same level of service to the overall population of patients. We are obviously very good at some things, e.g., surgery and research, but weak in others including preventative education and treatment, making sure that everybody has access to quality care, effective integration of our resources, protecting our providers in ways that best allows them to focus on their work, and designing efficiency into our system.

A lot of people argue that the concepts of universal healthcare and cost effectiveness/efficiency cannot be fit together, and that the two concepts are totally antithetical to each other. These people are wrong. In fact, according to information released by the World Health Organization (WHO) and a wide range of other organizations, universal systems in other countries have proven themselves to be much more cost effective than ours. The reasons are many, but a good starting point is that they are based on cooperation rather than competition and that, as a result, they are better integrated.

An obvious need exists to redesign our system, building it, once again, around the basic premise that healthcare should be a *right* rather than a *privilege*. In order to do this, one of the first things we should address is the question of finances. What is the best way to finance healthcare in the United States? How it is going to be paid for? Should it be entirely free, paid for with taxes? Should it be paid for through insurance, private or government sponsored? Should the patient be expected to pay a portion of the cost?

Also, how should we pay our healthcare providers? Should they all be on salary or should the level of payment be based on results? A number of different alternatives exist, especially concerning physicians. Some countries have all physicians on salary. In Italy, while general practitioners are paid on a capitation basis, specialists receive fee for service. At the same time, all physicians in Italy are eligible for government- and hospital-provided financial incentives. In France, both general practitioners and specialists are paid fee for service.

And what about insurance? What role should insurance play in the ideal system? Should insurance be controlled by the private sector, as it is now in this country, or should the government provide it? Finally, what about the system's customers? Should financial incentives exist for them as well, incentives that encourage them to take care of themselves, to stay healthy? Would this be a cost effective approach to dealing with the population's unwillingness or inability to practice prevention and to seek early treatment?

Lots of questions need to be addressed concerning the finances of our model. One way to begin addressing them is by benchmarking; in other words, looking around in an attempt to discover how other countries that treat healthcare as a right handle their system's finances, then picking a few with an approach judged more successful than ours and seeing how they do it and then studying the key elements of their model.

France

We shall begin again with France. Even though much has changed since the 2000 WHO rankings, many experts still consider its system to be among the best. French healthcare is part of its government's social security system. A majority of the funding comes from payroll taxes paid by employers. Much smaller amounts are gained from payroll taxes on employees and special taxes on automobiles, tobacco, and alcohol. Less than 1 percent comes from a specific tax on the pharmaceutical industry. The rest, around 30 percent, results from general revenue taxes, though this amount is growing due to the fact that the payroll taxes on employers act as a restraint to hiring and, therefore, are being reduced.[1]

The National Health Insurance Department (NHI) has been created to manage the healthcare domain in France. This department exercises its trusteeship through federal, regional, and departmental services. Each year, it presents a bill to the French Parliament seeking funds for the healthcare system. The bill includes a list of improvements it would like to make. How many of these improvements are funded depends, of course, on the amount of taxes raised that year.

The NHI administers the French healthcare system through three major funds and eleven smaller ones based on occupation.[2] The resistance of private insurance companies to the implementation of a universal healthcare system (UHS) was overcome in part by allowing them to administer these funds. The system allows all citizens access to treatment. Its success is evidenced in the general health of the French population, where overall life expectancy increases more than three months each year and where women have the second highest life expectancy rate in the world after Japan.

The French system is a combination of government funding that covers 75 percent of the total cost, supplemental insurance that covers roughly 12 percent of the remainder, and out-of-pocket monies spent to make up the difference when the universal system is being used. For those who are unemployed and cannot gain insurance through a family member, the government picks up the tab.[3]

French citizens using the UHS have the right to choose from healthcare providers in that sector. The 80 percent who also buy insurance sold by for-profit companies, however, have access to professionals working in the private sector as well as those working in the UHS. Most people take advantage of both sectors depending on what the problem is. The UHS is used for preventative care, for minor illnesses and injuries; the private sector is utilized for more complex problems like cancer treatment, intricate surgeries, and hard to define diseases.

As we have said, physicians can work either in the public sector or the private, but not in both. Fees for all UHS services are determined yearly by a board including representatives from the healthcare professions, the insurance fund, and the state. Physicians with their own practice collect these fees. Those working full time in public sector hospitals, along with the rest of the staff, are part of the civil service and, therefore, are on salary, with advancement and raises being based on seniority. Private sector doctors collect fees from private insurance companies and work with private for-profit and not-for profit hospitals that cater to patients with private insurance.

Patients must pay immediately out-of-pocket after receiving treatment in the French UHS. They are then reimbursed by the NHI department, any difference being made up by supplemental insurance if they possess it or out-of-pocket again if they don't. Making patients pay up front is thought to create a sense of responsibility and to cut down on unnecessary requests for treatment.

In contrast to the current U.S. system, one of the oddities of the French system is that "the sicker you are, the more coverage, care, and treatment you receive."[4]

Key Features of the French System

1. The government-supported segment is controlled by the NHI department and is part of social security. It is paid for mainly through payroll taxes, though this is shifting toward general tax revenues. The private segment is supported by private insurance.
2. Doctors can work either in the public sector or in the private sector, but they cannot work in both.
3. Patients with NHI insurance from one of the funds can go to any physician they want in the public sector. Patients with private insurance can go to any physician in either the UHS or the private sectors.
4. Public sector treatment is largely free. Patients typically use public sector services for preventative and low-level care, private sector services for surgery, cancer treatment, and other more sophisticated procedures. The private insurance system, therefore, complements rather than competes with the government-sponsored system.
5. All healthcare professionals in the public sector hospitals are government employees and are paid a salary. Physicians with a practice in the public sector collect fees. The wages of private sector professions are determined by the amount of insurance collected.
6. Patients using the public sector must pay for treatment out-of-pocket after receiving it. They are then reimbursed by the NHI department.
7. The sicker you are, the more free coverage you receive.

Germany

In France, all citizens are eligible for healthcare services sponsored by the NHI, and receive reimbursements from the NHI. A majority also purchases private insurance to help make up differences and to allow more specialized care when desired. In Germany, only about 10 percent of the population buys private insurance. This includes the wealthy and self-employed. These people share the same healthcare delivery system as the rest; the major difference is that they enjoy more amenities. The other 90 percent of the population gain access through a social insurance program that is funded by taxes and administered through more than 400 heavily regulated, fiscally independent, semiprivate, nonprofit "sickness funds."[5]

When a person joins one of these state-regulated sickness funds that are designed to meet a wide range of needs, the premium is set as a percentage of that person's job income. It ranges from approximately 9 to 17 percent, depending on the fund chosen. Approximately half of the involved premium is deducted from employee pay. The other half comes from the employer.

Revenues from fund premiums cover approximately 68 percent of the healthcare system's total costs. The remainder is covered by a combination of tax revenues, revenues from those with private healthcare insurance, and co-payments. Those over 65 years of age, as well as the unemployed, have their premium paid in full by the government.[6]

People who become members of funds are free to choose any physician they wish. However, the number of physicians allowed to practice in any neighborhood is regulated by the government. Physicians work on a fee-for-service basis, each fund setting its own fee schedule after negotiating it with the Medical Association and the government, so that it fits within the state budget. When treatment has been delivered, the professional bills the insurance fund directly.

A major difference between the German and French systems, therefore, is that, while in France one standard, universal set of fees has been set by the NHI, in Germany the fees for different procedures can vary according to the fund one belongs to.

Patients with private insurance are generally billed directly by healthcare providers. They are then reimbursed by the insurance company. Doctors can charge those with private insurance more, but the insurer can refuse to pay anything considered unreasonable.

Key Features of the German System

1. Healthcare for 90 percent of the population is paid for through government regulated "sickness funds." Private insurance also exists, but is only used by the other 10 percent. The two populations share the same services.

2. Approximately half of an insurance premium is paid for by employees through salary deduction, the size of the premium being based on the size of the salary being earned. The rest of the premium is paid for by the employer.
3. Charges are set for all procedures paid for through sickness funds, though these charges might vary according to the fund one belongs to. People using private insurance can be charged more, but the involved insurance company must be willing to accept the rate.
4. People belonging to a sickness fund may go to any provider they wish.
5. Because payment is received on a fee-for-service basis, how much healthcare professionals make depends on how many patients they treat and how much the involved fund pays.

Canada

In the Canadian system, each citizen is guaranteed comprehensive healthcare coverage by law. Control of the system has been delegated to the provincial governments. They have the power to decide how to support it. Premiums, payroll taxes, and sales taxes are some of the approaches used. The federal government contributes when the need arises. Canada is the only truly single payer system we have studied. Rather than government-supported funds, the government is the only source of payment for services rendered, with bills being submitted electronically.

Private insurance is also available. Eventually, the government tried to make its sale illegal, but a 2005 Canadian High Court decision refuted the government's argument; thus it remains legal. Obviously, Canada is moving toward the European model of both free government-funded insurance and available paid-for private insurance.

Practitioners work primarily in private practices and operate on a fee-for-service basis. After providing treatment to patients, the physician or facility makes electronic entries to province headquarters, or to the private insurance company, in order to receive payment. Caps for various procedures are set through negotiations between local medical associations and provincial government representatives. Obviously, they can differ. What will be paid by private insurance for a procedure is decided by the insurance company.

As a result of this arrangement, the amount of the payment doctors and other healthcare professionals receive depends on how many patients are seen and the nature of their ailments. Treatments considered unnecessary are not paid for by the province-sponsored insurance. These are usually paid for by private insurance or directly by the patient out-of-pocket.

The one exception concerning payment for services is that healthcare professionals working in outlying areas where few people live are on salary. This difference exists in order to attract them to such areas. Due to the smaller number of potential clients, they would make less if they were paid on the per-treatment basis.

The weaknesses of the Canadian system include the waiting period necessary after one makes an appointment. According to a Fraser Institute 2004 report, the average waiting time between referral from a general practitioner and treatment across the twelve specialties and ten provinces surveyed rose from 17.7 weeks in 2003 to 17.9 weeks in 2004.[6] Another weakness is the current shortage of technology available to practitioners, especially those who practice in the great expanses of near wilderness or wilderness that lies far from cities. A third current weakness, as in the United States, is the lack of emphasis on preventative care.

Key Features of the Canadian System

1. As in France and Germany, equal benefits are available to all citizens through a government-funded insurance program. Private insurance has also been made legal, but is currently held by a relatively small percentage of the population.
2. Probably because of the size of the country and the differences in population found, premiums and tax revenues needed to support the system are collected directly by and distributed directly from the provinces, rather than being collected by the centralized federal government and distributed from one location.
3. The cost of each procedure is negotiated between the provincial government and the local medical association. Procedures considered "not necessary" are not covered by the government insurance.
4. The approach is cost-effective because it is based on a single payer system, the payer being the province government.
5. Providers bill the province electronically, thus cutting down on paperwork.
6. Because professionals are paid on a fee-for-service basis, the number of patients they see determines the size of their salary.

Japan

The Japanese system is, again, considered one of the top in the world (ranked tenth by the WHO). Evidence of this includes the facts that Japan has the highest life expectancy rate and the lowest infant mortality rate in the world. Everybody is eligible for comprehensive care; wealth is not a factor. The Japanese approach to supporting healthcare is quite similar to that of the countries we have surveyed thus far. Expenditures are financed mainly through payroll taxes paid by employers and employees. In this country, however, the employee pays more than the employer, approximately 34 percent of the cost. The employer pays approximately 22 percent. With the exception of the roughly 12 percent of that comes out-of-pocket for treatment, the rest of the cost is subsidized by national and public funding.

If people in Japan hold a job or have money, they are required to hold insurance. A range of different plans exists to choose from including:

- Government-managed plans that cover approximately 30 percent of the working population plus their dependents.
- Society plans that cover approximately 25 percent of the working population and their dependents. These are controlled by representatives of labor and management.
- Mutual Aid Association Insurers that cover government employees and quasi-public employees like teachers.
- Plans for day laborers and seamen.[7]

While most of the involved plans are administered by private, nonprofit organizations, they are required to pay attention to government regulation. A schedule of fees for the services provided is set by a government-organized panel that includes insurers, providers, and citizens. Co-payments that frequently equal 30 percent of the bill are required. When patients seek treatment in a hospital, they are required to pay part of the fee in advance. They also must find a "sponsor" who signs an agreement to provide the co-pay if the patients fails to do so. Insurance for those who are unemployed or do not have money is arranged by the government. Finally, a scale has been established so that as the cost of procedures increase, the size of the co-pay decreases.

A major difference between the Japanese system and that found in the United States is that supplementary private insurance enjoys relatively little popularity in Japan. Less than 1 percent of the population subscribes to it.

Concerning specialists in clinics, they all receive the same fee for a given procedure, collecting the co-pay directly from the patient. As with other countries we have studied, the fee schedule is set. The Japanese schedule, however, is in most cases lower than that of the other countries. This arrangement encourages doctors to see as many patients as possible. While in the United States, it is estimated that physicians spend an average of twelve minutes with each patient, in Japan the same estimate is an average of three minutes, with physicians there seeing as many as one hundred patients daily. Also, this arrangement encourages excessive use of lab tests and technology. Finally, physicians in Japan can sell prescriptions directly to patients as a means of enhancing their income. Possibly as a result of this practice, Japan has the highest consumption rate of pharmaceuticals per capita in the world.

Doctors working in hospitals are on salary. The major problem in Japan at this point, one that costs the system dearly, is the average length of stay is hospitals, estimated by a contributing physician to be 40 days. This anomaly is largely a result of the aging population mentioned earlier. Traditionally, the Japanese have demonstrated a great deal of respect for their elders by keeping them at home where the wives would take care of them. But now that Japanese families are bearing fewer children, now that more women are entering the work force, it is becoming increasingly difficult to continue this practice.

Also, due at least partially to the long history of this tradition, until recently, relatively few nursing homes specializing in care for the aged have been built in Japan. Thus, the only place for them to go has been the hospital where many of them have stayed until they die, which places a large financial and workload burden on the healthcare system.

Key Features of the Japanese System

1. The system is financed mainly through payroll taxes with the employee paying a larger share than the employer.
2. Like the other healthcare systems surveyed, all citizens receive coverage, which is delivered by a four major insurance plans serving different segments of the population plus several smaller ones.
3. Unlike most of the other systems surveyed, private insurance does not play a major role. Those with private insurance also use UHS facilities and professionals.

4. All fees for all procedures are set by a government-organized panel including insurers, providers, and citizens.
5. Co-pays that cover 30 percent of the bill are required of patients. For high-cost procedures, this amount is reduced.
6. Patients entering a hospital have been required to find a "sponsor" who will agree to pay for the services delivered when the patient cannot.
7. When patients seek treatment in a hospital, they are expected to pay part of the bill in advance, with their insurance reimbursing them later.
8. Doctors in clinics work on a fee-for-service basis, which encourages them to treat as many patients as possible.
9. Physicians are allowed to sell medications directly to patients.
10. Physicians holding positions in hospitals are on salary.

Norway

Norway has the most centralized healthcare system of the countries we have discussed. Like Canada, it is single-payer. Policies and the yearly budget are set by the federal government. The system is financed by general tax revenue payments raised at the county level. All payments are made through the National Insurance Scheme from the county level rather than through a variety of different plans or funds. All citizens are covered. While there are small co-pays for outpatient treatment, there are none for hospital stays or drugs. Care can be denied if it is considered unnecessary.

Doctors in Norway are salaried and their salaries are based on the number of patients who have chosen them as their primary physician. Only specialists can work on a fee-for-service basis.

The major problem in Norway, again, is the waiting time for procedures. According to *Healthcare around the World: Norway,* approximately 23 percent of all patients referred for hospital treatment wait longer than three months for admission.[8] Private insurance does not exist. If patients do not want to wait, they can travel to another country and pay out of pocket.

Key Features of the Norwegian System

1. Policy is set by the national government.
2. All citizens are covered. The National Insurance Scheme, which is funded by general tax revenues, is the sole payer for medical claims.
3. No private insurance exists.

4. There are no fees for service except in the case of specialists. Small co-pays are required for outpatient care.
5. Doctor's salaries are based on the number of patients who have chosen them as a primary physician. This is the "capitation" system.

Interesting Comparisons

There are several interesting comparisons that can be made between the countries we have examined. Also, the United States will be included in our evaluation to see how we measure up.

In terms of how universal healthcare is paid for, Norway has a single-payer arrangement. County administrators raise the necessary taxes and make all payments through The National Insurance Scheme.

In Canada, which also has a single-payer arrangement, the provinces handle this chore. They raise the money through premiums, taxes, etc., and then redistribute it in the form of a government-sponsored insurance. As in Norway, the patient is not involved in the payment process. The physician submits a claim electronically and is paid directly by the provincial government.

The NHI in France makes all payouts from its budget, the funds coming mainly from social security taxes. A check is sent from one of the three major insurance funds with membership based on occupation or from one of the eleven smaller ones to reimburse the patient who has paid for the service immediately after receiving it.

Japan also bases its insurance breakdown on occupation. That country has four major plans that use money collected from occupation taxes to cover employees in four different sectors of the economy as well as their dependents. The patient or the patient's "sponsor" is responsible for covering up to 30 percent of the bill with a co-pay.

The United States also provides government funds for treatment. Five programs discussed in Chapter 2—Medicare, Medicaid, SCHIP, the VA, and Tricare—are funded by federal tax revenues and serve five different populations: people over 65, poor people, children whose parents can't afford private insurance but make too much to qualify for Medicaid, military veterans, and the families of soldiers on active duty. Physicians submit claims that are paid directly without any involvement of the patient.

Next comes Germany with a wide range of "sickness funds" that distribute government monies collected mainly through employment taxes. The purpose of this range of funds is to cover a wide variety of patients needs.

A second interesting comparison is the roll played by private insurance companies in these countries. At one end of the spectrum is Norway where one finds no private insurance. In Norway, all services are funded by the National Insurance Scheme. Anything a citizen wants that is not funded by this scheme must be paid for out-of-pocket.

Then comes Japan where less that 1 percent of the population buys supplemental private insurance. Everybody in Japan belongs to one of the government-regulated plans. While these plans are administered by private sector organizations, they are nonprofit and are strongly regulated. Everybody receives the same quality and type of care. There is no way to purchase something better, except, perhaps, by tipping the physician.

In the middle of the spectrum, we have France, Germany, and, more recently, Canada. In these countries, private insurance can be purchased and used if one is seeking a higher quality of care. In Canada, private insurance is still struggling to gain a foothold after the government failed in an attempt to eliminate it. In Germany, approximately 30 percent of the population has supplementary private insurance, though the government is trying to discourage its use. In France, approximately 80 percent of the population has private insurance that complements the UHS and is used for more specialized treatment.

At the other end of the spectrum, we have the United States where private, for-profit insurance dominates. Anybody not in one of the populations that qualify for our five federal programs needs private insurance in order to receive treatment. An estimated 47 million people lack such coverage either because they cannot afford it or because they have been denied coverage.

AN IDEALIZED FINANCE SYSTEM FOR A U.S. UHS

How the Necessary Monies Will Be Raised

Idealized design, as we have said, is a tool used by those who think systemically. Instead of starting where they are in efforts to improve a company, a program, a country, they start by identifying where there would like to be ideally, or what things would look like ideally if they could make changes today. Though ideals are, by definition, unreachable, such an exercise gives a target to aim for when the improvement effort actually begins.

Taking the best characteristics of the systems described above and adding some of our own, we will now try to put together what we consider an "ideal" way of financing a U.S. combined UHS/private healthcare system.

Funding for healthcare in the United States currently comes from three sources. The first is the individual's pocket or paycheck. Such payment is made either directly to the provider involved or to an insurance company that then pays (usually) the major part of medical expenses. The second source is employers who split the cost of medical insurance with employees. This insurance covers the major share of expenses for employees and their families while they are working and, sometimes, after they have retired. The third source is the federal government. Most of the funds from this source are used to support Medicare, Medicaid, the VA program, SCHIP, and Tristar.

Therefore, the key players in our system concerning funding are the individual citizen, the employer, insurance companies, and the government. In the French system, the same players exist, but whereas for-profit insurance companies dominate the U.S. system, they play a secondary role in France and are strongly regulated.

In the German system, insurance companies cater to only a relatively small percentage of the population including the extremely wealthy. The government is currently trying to reduce their role. In the Canadian system, they are just getting involved, and in Japan and Norway, they play little of no role whatsoever.

Funding for the "ideal" system we are designing will also come from several sources. The main source will be social security taxes levied on both employees and employers, as in France. This makes sense because our current government-funded programs—Medicare, Medicaid, VA, SCHIP, Tristar—are already part of the social security system. They will be rolled into the UHS and their administrations combined and reorganized to handle healthcare financing for the entire U.S. population rather than for just one segment of it. This way we will not need to develop a new channel, a new bureaucracy. Rather, we will be shrinking and gaining increased control over the bureaucratic "mess" that already exists.

As in other countries, monies from federal income tax will be added when necessary to meet budget requirements. The efficiencies of scale created by this move, the collapsing of regulations into one set, and the elimination of redundancies should create tremendous savings.

A smaller portion of the funding will come from sales tax on items defined as deleterious to health (tobacco, alcohol, etc.). Another part of the funding will be the monies paid for insurance policies.

Of course, the phrase "monies paid for insurance policies" brings up a critical question. Should our idealized system that is being designed in the belief that comprehensive healthcare should be a right and not a privilege, include access to private insurance? It plays a very small role or no role at all in two of the healthiest cultures in the world: Japan and Norway. But, then, a major problem in Norway, as with Canada, is that people are forced to wait in line, sometimes for months, in order to receive treatment.

The argument against allowing private insurance companies to remain in the game was recently repeated on the *Physicians for a National Health Program* Web site:

> Whenever we allow the wealthy to buy better care or jump the queue, healthcare for the rest of us suffers. If the wealthy are forced to rely on the same health system as the poor, they will use their political power to assure that the health system is well funded. Conversely, programs for the poor become poor programs. For instance, because Medicaid doesn't serve the wealthy, the payment rates are low and many physicians refuse to see Medicaid patients. Calls to improve Medicaid fall on deaf ears because the beneficiaries are not considered politically important.[9]

Also, in Italy where they have both a UHS and a private insurance-based system, where physicians are allowed to practice in both, the emphasis is apparently on attracting and treating patients with private insurance because the doctor gets paid more. In some cases, technology being paid for with universal system funds is being used to treat private sector patients as well.[11]

The counter-argument is that when competition with the private sector does not exist, the UHS tends to bog down, as it did in England before that country began allowing private insurance to be sold and used.

The country that seems to have discovered the best alternative is France. Perhaps this is part of the reason for its continued high ranking as a healthcare provider. The key seems to be that while both sectors (public and private) exist in France, physicians are allowed to practice in only one, and that the two sectors have come to a tentative understanding of which should focus on what.

Therefore, our idealized financing system will follow the French model in terms of private healthcare insurance. The hope will be that with the cost of malpractice insurance and education sharply reduced, with a physician incentive system based on capitation and prevention (we will talk about that later), not every medical school graduate will want to pile into the private sector.

How the Money Will Be Spent

Our healthcare service system will have three tiers. On the first tier, social security tax funds will cover the free provision of healthcare education and preventative services. On the second tier, these tax funds will also pay for what we call "necessary" care. Finally, on the third tier, insurance bought by individuals with possible assistance from employers will help cover "necessary" care the insurance holder wants from a private sector provider for a variety of reasons including unwillingness to wait for treatment in the government-supported system and the belief that the private practitioner is more skilled. It will also help cover treatment defined as "unnecessary." Individual employers will decide whether or not to pay for or to help employees pay for the insurance required for unnecessary healthcare services.

Canada collects and distributes its funds at the province level. Norway does so at the county level. In our system, the funds needed to support our idealized system will be collected at the national level (social security) as in France and Germany and distributed through the hierarchy of UHS Departments of Healthcare Administration. The federal UHS Board of Director's responsibilities in this model will include setting national policies concerning the distribution of UHS funds, facilitating integration and learning between the different states concerning distribution efforts, and funding emergency shortfalls.

Monies supporting the private part of the system will come solely from insurance premiums.

First tier educational and preventative services, as we have said, will be free and will be paid for directly from tax monies. A list of such services— education, testing, etc.—will be distributed to each individual and family. Based on client population (the necessary information being drawn from the regional computerized universal information system (UIS) data hub), preventative services will be delivered by local community health center staff. Each center will be allocated a yearly budget to support this work.

Second tier "necessary care" will be paid for from tax revenues through a yearly allowance allotted each citizen. The size of this allotment will be determined according to predefined factors, such as age, previous health record, and occupation, the information again drawn from the regional UIS data hubs. **Note:** If the allowance is not used entirely by the end of the year, the citizen will be allowed to keep one-half of the remainder. This will encourage people to take advantage of the free preventative services. It will also encourage people not to overuse the system, a major problem in other societies with universal healthcare.

Whereas responsibility for cutting down on over usage has traditionally been the responsibility of the medical and administrative staff, and has frequently led to a conflict situation (Patient: "Yes, I need this treatment." Medical staff: "No, you don't."), it will now rest with the patient ("If I show up for my scheduled physical examinations, if I do the exercises recommended, if I take the medication prescribed, I might be able to cut down on the number of visits to the clinic necessary and make some money) leading to a win–win situation.

If, on the other hand, the individual depletes his or her allowance and needs more, due, perhaps, to a chronic illness or to a serious injury, additional costs will be covered by a catastrophic fund administered from the state level by the state UHS Department of Healthcare Administration.

All patient co-payments will be eliminated, which, again, will simplify the administrative process. In order to be eligible for their allowance, people will be required, as in Norway, to register with a primary care physician. They can pick any one they wish. Community health center physicians will be required to include a certain percentage from five age brackets—children, teenagers, young adults, adults, the elderly—in their patient population when possible. The physician will schedule their patients for a free physical examination every six months. If the person misses the examination, he or she will be docked a predefined amount from his or her allowance unless a good excuse is offered. In such cases, the examination will be rescheduled. If the person misses again, he or she will be docked again. This cycle will continue until the person comes in.

When the patient is diagnosed with an illness or injury and an appointment is made for treatment, it will, again, be the patient's responsibility to show up. If the patient does not and lacks a good excuse, that person's allowance also will be docked, thus cutting their year-end reward.

One of the responsibilities of the social worker on a community health center physician's team will be to get to know patients, to learn their family and work situation, to keep track of their appointments for checkups and treatment, and to encourage patients in any way possible to meet these appointments. Social workers on the teams of specialized clinic physicians will have the same responsibilities.

This approach, of course, raises hackles. "People shouldn't have to be bribed to get them to do what is good for them," I hear. The reply must be, "Yes, this can be called a bribe. Yes, it will cost some money up front. But, in the long term the benefit should be obvious—less illness, less hospitalization, more productivity. In the long term, the benefit of this approach will far outweigh the cost." So, our question in return must be, "Which is more important, making sure nobody gets a handout or saving money for tax payers?"

What this approach does is to redefine the profit motive in healthcare. Rather than benefiting at other people's expense, the key players involved will benefit solely by improving the health of the populace. Patients will benefit financially by staying healthy and by becoming healthy when they are sick through their bonus. Medical professionals, as we learn later in this chapter, will benefit financially by keeping their charges healthy. The community will benefit by having fewer people miss work. The UHS will benefit through reduced cost. And, ultimately, the taxpayer will benefit by having to pay less taxes to support the system.

What has been designed, it turns out, is a win-win-win-win-win, profit-driven alternative.

Payment for services judged unnecessary will come from private sector insurance purchased by the individual, from insurance paid for by the employer, or from a combination of both. It can also, of course, come out-of-pocket. What is "necessary" and what is "unnecessary" will be defined by the UHS Board of Directors at the state level in that it might differ from state to state.

While the cost for every treatment will be set in the UHS, no caps will exist in the private sector. Laissez-faire economics will rule. If the cost of a procedure in the private sector is too high or if private insurance will not or does not cover it, people will still be able to return to the UHS when the treatment is deemed "necessary."

The UHS payment system, therefore, has four levels. On the first level, we find the government paying directly for educational services and for free preventative services. On the second level, we find necessary services paid for from the individual's tax-supported allowance. On the third level, additional necessary services are paid for through the catastrophic fund once an individual's allowance has been depleted. On the fourth level, we find services deemed unnecessary paid for through private sector insurance or out-of-pocket.

Because the unemployed are not paying taxes that feed the system, they will be required to *earn* their healthcare benefits. This will be done through community service of some sort. A certain number of hours will be spent delivering healthcare education, assisting at a community health center, working with children in daycare centers, working with the elderly in retirement and nursing homes, or helping out at a local school or a youth center. The assignments will be identified and coordinated by a local community health center staff member, most likely a social worker. Some of these assignments might lead to employment.

Compensation for Healthcare Providers

Now comes the tricky part. The cost for necessary services and procedures in the UHS (the second tier) will be set at the regional level by the Regional UHS Board of Directors. Usually, the cost will be the same across all regions. Patients will pay for these services from their allowance. The healthcare facility will electronically submit a bill to the UIS hub at the regional level of the UHS. The amount will be electronically deducted from the patient's allowance or from the catastrophic fund when no more funds are left in an allowance. If there is money left in the patients allowance at the end of the year, the patient receives half as a reward for focusing on prevention and staying healthy.

But, how do we incentivize professionals in the UHS, especially at the entry level, the community health center level? How do we encourage them to focus on keeping their clients healthy, to focus on prevention? If doctors and their teams are paid in the traditional manner, if their salary depends on the number and types of treatments administered, then emphasis will be on quantity rather than quality; the health centers and staffs will need to treat a lot of patients in order to bring in a lot of money.

From a common sense perspective, this arrangement does not encourage prevention. In fact, it encourages just the opposite; the more illness there is, the more money you make. Also, speed becomes more important than thoroughness.

On the other hand, if we put staff on salary, say, make them civil service employees, we risk killing incentive. Quite simply, why should I work hard when I am going to make the same amount seeing 100 patients as I will seeing just 10? Also, while preventative education is no longer a hindrance to improving my compensation, "Why should I put much effort into it? Whether I educate my patients or not, I still get paid the same amount."

So, what we need in our idealized design of a UHS is to find something in the middle, an approach that encourages thoroughness, but, at the same time, one that does not kill incentive; an approach that encourages staff to push prevention as an alternative so patients don't have to keep coming back, thus, saving money for the UHS system.

In order to get where we want to go, we need to think outside the box. We need to shift our focus from the healthcare network we are building to the targeted population. We must begin with the result we want to achieve and work backward. The result we want to achieve in this instance is that patient use of the healthcare network decreases because people are getting healthier. They are getting healthier because community health center staff is doing a continually better job of educating and treating them.

However, there is a problem with this thinking. If community health center staff succeeds in keeping clients healthy so that they don't need treatment, aren't the staff members working themselves out of a job?

In our idealized model, as in France, doctors will choose to work in the UHS sector or the private sector, but not in both. We have learned from the Italian experience that allowing them to work in both creates problems. Concerning payment for services, the community center physicians and their teams will be paid salaries based on seniority and on a capitation system. As we have said, in order to qualify for their UHS allowance, citizens must enroll with a primary physician. As in Norway, they will be allowed to change their choice twice during the year if unsatisfied. The salaries of physicians and their teams will be based *not* on the number of services delivered, but on the number of people who have enrolled with them. Salaries will be adjusted biyearly as a result of changes in this number.

Professionals who work on more than one team, say, nutritionists, will add the number of patients enrolled in all the teams involved, then will divide that number by the number of teams. This will be the figure that salary adjustments are based on. Professionals rotating between centers and not teams, say, health educators, will be on straight salary based on years of service.

Up to this point, what we are putting into place is basically the Danish reimbursement system. But, that is where the similarity ends. The Danish system gives incentive to attract as many patients as possible. By keeping one's patients healthy, the physician attracts more patients and, thus, gets paid more. There is an emphasis on prevention, but in order to strengthen that emphasis, we shall add another reward. In order to incentivize the physician teams to do the things we want them to do, we will cut them into the savings accrued by their encouragement of prevention and early treatment.

As we have said, half of the patient's allowance not spent will go to the patient. The other half will be returned to the government at the end of the year (actually, it will not have been distributed) and will be divided in half again. One-half of this amount will be added to the catastrophic fund. The logic behind this decision is that while people are younger and need less healthcare, they will be investing money in the catastrophic fund that will help support them when they are older and need more care. In other words, when they are more likely to deplete their yearly allowance and need assistance from the fund.

The second half of this amount (half of the patient's allowance not spent) will be returned to the community health center. At the center, it will again be divided. One-half of what is returned will be awarded to the physician's team in the form of a bonus for a job well done. The other half will go into a pot to be split equally among all center employees at the end of the year.

So, we have discovered a way in which, rather than losing their jobs, staff are rewarded for emphasizing prevention. They will be rewarded because, as we have said, all citizens will be required to register with a community health center, no matter what the state of their health, and to show up for mandatory six-month checkups. Every citizen will receive an allowance. Community health center employees, therefore, will actually be rewarded with a bonus for decreasing the need to spend this allowance, for decreasing the need to utilize center services.

In order to help make clear what is being proposed, let's give an example. The average 2008 per capita cost for healthcare in the United States was $6,400, which was approximately double that for any other country.[10] So, in that the UHS being designed is going to function more efficiently than our current system, we will make the yearly allowance $2,500 for a healthy ten-year-old. In the best-case scenario, due to the preventative care delivered, all this child will need are the two required yearly physicals and treatment for a sinus infection, which adds up to less than $500. The remaining $2,000 will be divided, half going to the child, half being returned to the government. The $1,000 going to the government will again be divided, $500 being added to the catastrophic fund, $500 going back to the community health center where the child is enrolled. There, at the center, the $500 received will be divided. Two hundred and fifty dollars of it will go to the physician treatment team responsible for the child; the other $250 will go into the center pot to be divided among all center staff. Rotating professionals will be cut in on this part of the bonus.

Does this scenario make sense? Yes, it does. It makes a lot of sense because the circle is now complete. All three key stakeholder groups are focused on prevention, on keeping the population served healthy, and on returning patients to health as quickly as possible when they become sick or injured. The patient now has a monetary incentive to stay well, or when injured or ill to do what is necessary to heal. Staff in the system now also has a monetary incentive to keep the population served as healthy as possible. And, finally, the government-funded UHS has a monetary incentive to facilitate these efforts.

The model gets rid of all possible conflicts in terms of objectives. It incorporates pieces of the French, German, Canadian, Japanese, and Danish models. But it goes beyond, adding features that we believe make universal healthcare a more attractive alternative.

The earning of specialists and their teams working in specialized clinics will be based on a fee-for-service schedule set out, again, by the Regional UHS Board of Directors. No bonus will be earned because the emphasis here will be on curing those sent to the clinic, rather than on prevention. Physicians working in hospitals will be civil service employees paid a set salary based on skill level and seniority.

In terms of pensions, all UHS employees will be considered government employees and will be working toward a government pension.

Physicians who opt to serve in the private sector will submit bills directly to the insurance companies selected by their patients. The physicians can charge whatever they wish, but must negotiate fees with the insurance company involved, the company having the right to refuse what it considers an over-charge. Physicians can also require co-pays from patients. The realization that for-profit healthcare providers and for-profit insurance companies are entirely dependent on each other for survival, especially now that they have competition from the UHS, will help keep the prices charged by both lower.

For-profit healthcare organizations must pay staff salaries themselves. They must also find a facility outside the UHS network and pay for rent, equipment, and maintenance. They must also provide employee benefits. Private sector practitioners cannot charge the UHS for services rendered, which means that people without private insurance or unwilling to pay out-of-pocket cannot use them.

Citizens, of course, may use their yearly UHS allowance bonus the following year to help pay for private insurance. Those holding private insurance, as we have said, can still make use of the UHS. Thus, if they take advantage of the UHS for the "basics" (prevention, scrapes, and colds, etc.) and the private sector for more demanding ailments as the French do, their year-end bonus should be larger.

REFERENCES

1. The Health Care System under French National Insurance: Lessons for Health Reform in the United States, V. Rodwin, *American Journal of Public Health*, January 2003, 93 (1) 31–27.
2. The French Health Care System: Organization and Functioning, Marc Duriez, *Paris: CREDES*, 1994.
3. The French Lesson in Health Care, *Business Week*, July 9, 2007.
4. France's Model Healthcare System, Paul V. Dutton, *The Boston Globe*, August 11, 2007.
5. Germany's Health Care System: It's Not the American Way, Uwe E. Reinhardt, *Health Affairs*, Fall 1994.
6. Healthcare in Germany, Sue Grant, *Medhunters Magazine*, Spring 2003.
7. Waiting Your Turn: Hospital Waiting Lists in Canada, *Fraser Institute's 14th Annual Edition*, Vancouver, BC, 2004.
8. Comparing Health Care Systems: What Makes Sense for the U.S.? Ed Cooper, Liz Taylor, *Good Medicine*, Fall 1994.
9. Physicians for a National Health Program: http://www.nphp.org: (accessed February 2009).
10. Italy's Public Health-Care System Is Doing Poorly, *The New York Times*, Alan Cowell, January 1, 2009, A3.

5

Network Universal Information System

THE CHALLENGE

Proponents of linking all parts of the U.S. healthcare sector together with a universal information system (UIS) have recently begun working on a comprehensive alternative to the current approach. They have realized that the long-term benefits of a universal system will far outweigh the short-term cost and inconvenience. Such a system will improve communication and coordination between the full range of providers, ensuring that the necessary information is available wherever and whenever it is required. Such a system will lower costs by reducing medical errors. It will increase efficiencies, reduce duplication of efforts, and reduce paperwork. Such a system will improve research and facilitate the practice of evidence-based medicine.

The up-front cost of implementing such a system, however, remains an obstacle. It has been estimated that the cost will run between $75 billion and $100 billion, approximately half of this amount being spent on the development of a central database, complete with safeguards and oversight, to house mainly electronic health records (EHR).[1]

A second major problem identified has been the lack of interconnectedness of the many systems currently in place. There are physician's offices and clinics, hospitals, emergency medical services, homecare, long-term care, billing, scheduling and registration, pharmaceutical, laboratory, radiology, electronic medical records systems, computerized physician order entry, electronic claims submission, eligibility verification, and many other systems that do not currently communicate with each other effectively, if at all.

At the same time, due to the competition among the firms providing this technology, little incentive exists to develop the desired interconnectedness. There are currently a great number of niche software companies in the United States. For example, some specialize in emergency department charting, some in critical care, as well as some in medication reconciliation/discharge instructions. As a result, different departments in the same hospital quite frequently purchase their technology from different vendors who have tailored products to meet specific needs. The sacrifice made by doing so is that, while satisfactorily meeting these specific needs, the systems frequently cannot communicate adequately with other departments, thus hampering the overall effectiveness of the operation.

This problem gets worse when we talk about communication between hospitals and between departments treating similar illnesses in different hospitals. Getting individual practices and hospitals to share data and information with each other has frequently been difficult when they are battling for patients. This is at least partially due to the previously mentioned competitive atmosphere found in the healthcare sector to territorial issues found within individual hospitals as well as between hospitals.

A third major problem has to do with security. At this point, two critical concerns exist. One is the Health Information Portability and Accountability Act (HIPAA), a set of federal guidelines that limit the disclosure of health information, most importantly, medical records. This, of course, would present a barrier to the sharing of information when such sharing is critical to the success of a UIS as a critical part of a universal healthcare system (UHS).

Also, a critical concern is theft of medical identity and medical records.

All three of these obstacles can be overcome. Concerning cost, we learned in Chapter 2 that the overall cost of our current healthcare system per person, excluding start-up expenses, is almost double that of countries with universal programs in place. An addendum to this realization is that, despite the fact that they don't spend as much, the information part of the system in these countries is generally more advanced than ours. At the same time, the computer technology involved is becoming cheaper. According to Gordon Moore, co-founder and former CEO of Intel Corporation, while the power of the microchip doubles approximately every eighteen months, the cost remains constant.[2]

Concerning interconnectedness, two approaches are possible. One is for the National Board of Directors to mandate that all healthcare network facilities utilize the same model, so that the ability to communicate is assured. The weakness with this setup, of course, is that it eliminates competition when competition is important to the encouragement of innovation. The second approach is for the National Board of Directors to produce a set of specifications that all UIS technology must meet and for the local boards of directors to oversee the purchase, implementation, and upgrading of technology in their network facilities to make sure it meets these specifications.

Concerning the territorial issues and concerning the unwillingness to share, the absence of the profit motive in a UHS coupled with government control over facility placement helps get rid of competitive impulses.

Finally, concerning theft of medical identity and medical records, multiple layers of protection will exist.

1. A firewall will protect the central database and all electronic information systems online.
2. Data being stored, manipulated, and transferred will be encrypted.
3. An automatic backup system will exist.
4. More than one layer of redundancy will be put in place. This will be made easier by the fact that we are not designing the central repository as one server sitting in a shed somewhere, tied to one location. Rather, we are designing the central repository as a complex system of connected "nodes" spread across the nation (the world?) that continually collects, stores, and transmits data in real time.
5. Different levels of access to health information will exist. System administrators will have the access necessary to run, update, and troubleshoot the system. Physicians and other healthcare workers will be allowed access to patient-related information based on their need to know. Researchers whose projects have been improved by a board of directors will also be allowed access on a need-to-know basis.
6. Physicians will be allowed to release information they believe appropriate to patients—medication lists, problem lists, laboratory and diagnostic tests, treatment plans.

At the same time, research shows that security is not as much of an issue in European countries, where the role of private insurance companies has been greatly reduced and where healthcare facilities are not competing and are not charging for their services. Medical theft is generally driven by the profit motive or by the desire of those involved in the delivery of healthcare not to spend money.

‎------

INFORMATION SYSTEMS IN OTHER COUNTRIES WITH UHS

But, again, before designing our ideal UIS for the United States, we will look to see what other countries have in place. In terms of centralizing their UHS information system, Canada and most European nations have developed or are in the process of developing the necessary vehicle. In most of these cultures, the central data bank is found on a national level, while in some, such as Canada, regional data banks have been established. One reason the challenge is more easily met in these countries is that private insurance companies are not involved as middlemen. The number of required communication channels, therefore, is smaller, as well as the number of requirements in terms of what information must be transferred and to whom.

In Europe, while individual nations are working to standardize and integrate the flow of healthcare information internally, an effort has also begun to standardize and integrate it on a continentwide basis, thus further facilitating the sharing of resources. But, let's start with Canada.

Canada

In 2000, the central government of Canada joined with its ten provincial and three territorial governments to develop an infostructure that would control, coordinate, and disseminate all health-related information electronically. The EHR system will enable the sharing of patient background information, charts, and test results by professionals in hospitals, labs, doctor's offices, and other care facilities all over the nation.[3]

Although these records are and will be housed in regional data warehouses rather than at one central national storage site, the federal government will still have access to them, using data gleaned to determine and help meet the needs of particular geographic areas or of the country as a whole.

As part of this project, seven rural health districts in the province of Alberta have announced an effort to standardize the format of patients' electronic health records. Efforts are also being made to implement an electronic medication record that will allow physicians to place pharmaceutical orders online. This approach streamlines the workflow process and minimizes the possibility of transcription errors, thus reducing paperwork and cost.

As another part of the project, the province of Alberta has created the world's first regional chronic disease management system called the Chronic Disease Management Infostructure (CDMI). Proper use of the involved information will help reduce costs in a segment of the population that in the United States, according to a 2003 survey by the American Medical Association, accounted for 67 percent of all healthcare spending.[4]

Key Features of the Canadian UHS Approach to Information

1. The federal and regional governments are coordinating efforts to develop a universal system.
2. The primary objective is to generate electronic health records for all citizens using a standardized format, these records being stored in regional data banks.
3. The federal government will have access to data stored in regional banks for research purposes.
4. Physicians have the ability to check medication records and to order medications for patients online.
5. A Chronic Disease Management Infostructure (CDMI) is being created to facilitate efforts to predict trends and allocate resources in the most effective manner, among other things, for Canadians suffering from chronic disease.

Great Britain

Britain's National Health Service (NHS) has awarded approximately $5 million in contracts to develop a lifelong EHR system for the approximately 50 million patients, 30,000 doctors, and 270 healthcare facilities involved.[5] Local service providers are being contracted to build their piece of the standardized information technology. The NHS will then link these pieces nationally. Such centralization will reduce costs by eliminating fragmentation and repetition in both paper and computer-based records. It will also, obviously, save a great deal of time.

National programs have been implemented to promote the use of this EHR system with a focus on primary care at the community center level. Basic patient information, including birth and death notifications, treatment records, medication records, allergy recording, and trips to the hospital, is included. Currently, 90 percent of all general practitioners are computerized and are working toward joining the EHR network.[6] An increasing number of physicians use electronic record systems for prescription purposes and nearly 30 percent state that their practices are paperless. It is hoped that by the year 2010 the EHR system will be in place and accessible across the country.[7]

In another project called the Electronic Health Record Demonstrator Implementation Project (EHRDIP), efforts are being made to include data from other community social service agencies dealing directly or indirectly with healthcare issues in the regional EHR bank and to allow those agencies access to the records.

While a majority of British information technology strategies are being developed by the national government, implementation remains on a regional/localized level. Going the other way, while funding for healthcare technology initiatives is distributed at the regional level, the national government also provides financial rewards for those general practices whose information systems meet national standards.

Although most of Britain's initiatives thus far have been geared toward increasing the efficiency of physicians, efforts are also underway to involve patients more directly and to provide more end-user services. One of these efforts is called the *NHS Direct*. This is a telephone service staffed by nurses and backed by decision support software. The service is currently available to two-thirds of the United Kingdom's 59 million population. It advises patients whether to treat themselves, to see the family doctor, or to call an ambulance.[8] An offshoot of the *NHS Direct* is the *NHS On-Line*, a computerized service that provides similar advice and receives nearly 100,000 hits per day. These two forms of assistance obviously help cut down on the number of patient visits to healthcare facilities.

NHS Net is another information technology development that enables the physician not only to communicate with health authorities when they have a question, but to book appointments for patients, to order tests from pathology labs, and to call up results.

Key Features of the British UHS Approach to Information

1. The federal government is leading the effort to develop a national healthcare strategy.
2. Regions are developing their own parts of the information system that are required to meet national standards and that will then be linked by the NHS.
3. All healthcare practitioners are working to become computerized and, eventually, paperless. Those who meet national standards are rewarded financially.
4. The primary objective is to generate electronic health records for all citizens, which will be stored in a data bank and can be accessed by physicians electronically.
5. Efforts are being made to include data from other social service agencies relevant to healthcare in the UHS bank and to give these agencies access to the bank.
6. Telephone and online services have been installed that help patients define the severity of their ailment and that encourage them to at least begin with home treatment.

Germany

Germany spends approximately 8.6 percent of its healthcare budget annually on technological innovation.[9] While an electronic health record system has been in place for years, a more advanced architect is being developed to provide increased security concerning the communication of patient and physician information.

At the same time, two "smart cards" are being researched. The first, the Electronic Health Card (EHC), will replace the card currently being used by patients. It will hold the patient's identification and parts of that person's electronic health records. It will provide cryptographic algorithms for authentication and digital signatures. This card will also hold part of the patient's personal prescription information.

The second smart card, known as the Healthcare Practitioner's Card (HPC), will contain the same security and authenticating codes as EHCs. It will be given to doctors, nurses, pharmacists, and other medical personnel with a need to know, allowing them access to patient medical and pharmaceutical records.

Once the two smart cards are in place, Germany plans for its national healthcare system to become entirely paperless. The electronic health record system will use two modules. The first will control applications, and the second will be a driver to facilitate efforts by smart card holders to access and manipulate data.

The electronic health record is designed to be multitier, ensuring scalability, security, and cleanliness of information movement. As a further precaution, all entries into the system, no matter what their purpose, will be logged into a database so that they can be traced.

Additional developments in Germany's system include the increased use of smart mobile medical devices and the provision of appliances needed to monitor patients being treated or observed at home.

Key Features of the German UHS Approach to Information

1. Germany is working to increase security in the country's electronic health record system.
2. The government is developing an electronic health card (Smart) for citizens that will allow them access to necessary information contained in their electronic health record.
3. The government is developing a similar Smart card for healthcare practitioners that will allow access to the patient's electronic health record.
4. Home monitoring devices are being distributed that cut down on the amount of time spent in hospitals and on the number of visits to clinics by recuperating patients.

Spain

On May 28, 2003, a nationally coordinated effort called the Cohesion and Quality of the National Health System went into effect. This system was designed to ensure that healthcare is provided throughout the country and that information technology is used effectively to facilitate the involved effort. The central government established regional offices authorized to modify systems based on local needs. Infrastructure and privacy issues are currently being researched. The common, binding vision of the project is to promote:

1. Patient-centered care
2. A decentralization of services

3. Constant improvement of processes
4. More autonomy for healthcare professionals

Healthcare facilities are being networked to allow the flow of patient data through the system in a seamless, integrated fashion. The growing use of wide-band access to the Internet has increased the potential of this e-Health approach. Traditional hospitals are being modernized with information technologies as a major concern, the new generation emerging as paperless. Emphasis is on improving the continuity of care between primary providers and hospitals.[10]

Other Spanish initiatives currently being tested in different regions include:

1. A national electronic health card similar to Germany's "smart" card
2. Telemedicine
3. Home care applications
4. An electronic prescription plan

One of Spain's initial innovations was a two-dimensional bar code technology developed as part of a new automated system for processing prescriptions nationwide. This system has improved the accuracy and efficiency of prescription reimbursement, lowered operating costs, and reduced prescription fraud.

Roadblocks to the full integration of Spain's healthcare information system are similar to those encountered in other European countries. One is the establishment of compatibility and interoperability between the technologies and policies found in different regions. A second roadblock concerns security and confidentiality requirements, especially when the international transfer of patient information is involved (between Spain and Germany, for instance). An effort is being made to develop international standards for such transfers.

Key Features of the Spanish UHS Approach to Information

1. The federal government is putting into place regional offices and encouraging them to be innovative and to modify their information system to meet local needs.
2. Emphasis is on making interactions between primary providers and hospitals as smooth as possible.

3. Hospitals are striving to become paperless.
4. The Internet is being used as a source of healthcare information.
5. A two-dimensional bar code technology for pharmaceuticals is increasing the efficiency of prescription processing and is lowering costs.

Sweden

Information technology in Sweden's healthcare system is currently, by international standards, at a highly integrated level. According to a Harris Interactive Survey, roughly 98 percent of general practitioners in Sweden have computerized practices, 3 percent use PDAs (personal digital assistants), 93 percent use the Internet or a general practitioner network, 90 percent utilize electronic medical records, and 42 percent have a Web site. In contrast, when we look at European Union general practitioners as a whole, approximately 80 percent have a computerized practice, 11 percent use a PDA, 61 percent use the Internet, 29 percent use electronic medical records, and 13 percent have a practice Web site. In the United States, most of these percentages are even lower, as one would expect.[11]

The establishment of the *Guide to Healthcare*, an Internet portal, provides Swedish patients with a wide range of healthcare information. If the *Guide* leads people to suspect that treatment is necessary, a personalized computer, cell phone, or WAP (wireless application protocol) device can be used to ask questions of a chosen physician, to voice concerns, or to make an appointment. Once the appointment is scheduled, patients can grant the physician access to preparatory information about weight, their medical history, the current condition of their health, their use of pharmaceuticals, etc., which are stored in their electronic medical record.

Identifiers exist to ensure security of the data being transmitted. The patients' ability to provide information of this type before the visit reduces the amount of paperwork required once they enter the office. This practice cuts administrative costs and the length of visits. It also allows more time to be spent in diagnosis and treatment.

The plan is that all patients will eventually carry Smart cards, similar to those used in Germany, with the cards allowing both the patient and the involved practitioner access to electronic medical records.

Sweden's vision is one of "instant mobility that relies on IT (information technology) to make all kinds of clinical patient information readily available to any healthcare provider anywhere who requires access to it in order to deliver effective treatment."[12]

Key Features of the Swedish UHS Approach to Information

1. Sweden makes greater use of electronic technology in its UHS than any other nation, the technology helping to cut long-term costs.
2. An Internet portal, *Guide to Healthcare*, has been established for public use.
3. If the decision is made by those using the *Guide to Healthcare* that more information is required or that care by a professional is necessary, a personalized computer, phone, or WAP device can provide immediate contact with the chosen physician.
4. Necessary information can be provided to a physician before the visit from the patient's electronic medical record or through the patient's Smart card so that during the visit less time is spent on paperwork and more is spent on treatment.
5. The developmental focus in Sweden is on increasing the mobility of information, on increasing its ability to be accessed immediately by different organizations, and by individual practitioners in any part of the healthcare network.

IDEALIZING A UHS INFORMATION SYSTEM FOR THE UNITED STATES

The countries we have talked about are all moving toward a computerized, centralized information system. Use of the Internet, the design and building of centralized data banks, the development of Smart cards that give both patients and professionals access to electronic health records, and the ability of citizens to interact electronically with healthcare providers is reducing costs while, at the same time, increasing the amount of care available. The quality of healthcare should also improve due, in part, to the amount and scope of data provided by federal and/or regional data banks. This data can be used both for patient visit preparation and for research. Errors will be detected more rapidly in an automated system, thus, again, improving the quality of healthcare statistics.

The use of other electronic information dispersing and gathering technology, such as telemedicine and home monitoring cameras, further facilitates treatment and reduces costs by giving patients an alternative to visiting the doctor or filling a hospital bed.

In order to support the UHS we are designing for the United States, the idealized information system must possess the following characteristics. It must:

1. Enable healthcare providers to gain relevant information on patients immediately.
2. Enable healthcare providers to gain relevant information on treatments immediately.
3. Enable healthcare providers to contact each other when necessary.
4. Allow patients direct access to their health records including all interactions with general practitioners, specialists, as well as to a history of medications.
5. Provide citizens with direct and immediate advice on healthcare concerns through the Internet.
6. Encourage and support preventative measures and self-treatment.
7. Enable healthcare providers to monitor the condition of patients at risk while the patients remain in their homes.
8. Enable healthcare providers to consult with patients without having them present physically.
9. Allow healthcare professionals to research family histories.
10. Allow healthcare professionals to research health-related trends in a wide range of populations including the poor, the wealthy, pregnant women, the elderly, those who have contacted a specific disease, those who have received a specific treatment or medication, and then to cross correlate the data.

Integration Is the Key

The universal healthcare system designed in this book combines the myriad systems currently in place in the United States into just one. This includes systems found in private physicians' offices and hospitals, community health centers and their satellites, specialized clinics, general hospitals, research/teaching/medical hospitals, nursing homes, independent research facilities, pharmacies, and support laboratories. The UIS will be built around a network of centralized, interactive databanks located in the regions defined earlier. For a system this large to function in the most effective manner, such a "nodular" approach is most appropriate. For one thing, it will provide consistent redundancy, so that if one regional node goes down, say, due to a natural disaster, another will be able to continue providing services to that region. National, state, and local boards of directors, as well as national, state, and local administrative offices will be part of this network, having access to any information required to meet responsibilities.

As with all the countries discussed thus far, the core data element around which the information system is built will be the individual electronic medical record (EMR). Efforts to generate such a record began in the United States during the late 1980s with the formation of Health Level Seven (HL7), a group whose goal was to create a standard protocol for interoperability among healthcare information systems. Fourteen people from various industries defined the group's mission. This mission was to provide a comprehensive framework along with specifications for the exchange, integration, storage, and retrieval of health information. Specifically, the group was formed to create flexible, cost-effective approaches; standards; guidelines; and methodologies to make sure that interoperability existed among the healthcare information systems being put in place and to do the same for the management of electronic health records.

HL7 membership now numbers over two thousand. The protocol developed by the organization has been chosen as the standard for information interchange among different information systems/data sources (ICD, CPT, LOINC, NDC). The first version of the protocol, 2.1, was released in 1990, and by 1998 it was being used by more than 95 percent of U.S. hospitals with four hundred or more beds. The latest version, 3.0, is known as HL7 XML. It is being developed to serve as the foundation for a universal electronic medical records system for the entire country.

The movement received a boost in 1996 with passage of the previously mentioned Kassebaum–Kennedy Act, also known as HIPAA. This event provided the first official recognition by the federal government that e-Commerce needed to play a role in healthcare.[13] The purpose of this legislation, besides protecting the individual's medical records, was to make it easier for those who changed jobs to retain health benefits by making them more portable from employer to employer (and to protect the records). It did so by creating federal standards for formatting transactions and for coding both clinical and financial information that is transmitted electronically.

A second boost to the movement came in 1999 with the release of the Institute of Medicine report, *To Err Is Human: Building a Safer Health System*, which claimed that most medical errors, including those in prevention, diagnosis, treatment, and the communication of important information, result from faulty technical systems rather than from negligent practitioners. This report claimed that as few as 48,000, and as many as 98,000, people die each year because of medical error at a cost of $37.6 billion to society. It also estimated that as many as one out of every twenty-five hospital patients suffers injury resulting from medical error or an adverse event (an injury caused by medical mismanagement).[14]

Then, in May of 2004, President Bush put his support behind the concepts of electronic medical records and a paperless system. The plan was to implement such a system nationwide. To facilitate this effort, the president created the position of National Health Information Technology Coordinator within the department of Health and Human Services (HHS). The goal was to implement a National Health Information Network by the year 2014.[15] Money was allocated to fund a project to harmonize standards for electronic health information exchange, for a project to develop certification standards, for one to address privacy and security issues, and, finally, to develop a model for a national Web-based health IT system.

Next, in 2007, President Bush proposed the development of nationwide standards in order to accelerate patient access to EHRs. Each EHR would include a "medical clipboard" that could be accessed by providers with the patient's consent, an electronic medication history, and lab test results. At the same time, the president encouraged the development of procedures allowing the utilization of health information tools to monitor disease outbreaks.

The HHS also spun off an advisory committee to begin the process of developing universal standards for electronic record generation and exchange, for laboratory results to be sent electronically, for biosurveillance, medications, quality measures, home health device monitoring, immunizations, genomic data, hospital to hospital transfers including imaging data, public health reporting, and patient provider secure messaging.

In 2006, The Markle Foundation's Connecting for Health project developed a prototype for interstate exchange of electronic health information, allowing facilities in Boston, Indianapolis, and Mendocino County, California, to communicate using the same database.

Weaknesses of Our Current Approach

Obviously, a lot is already happening, most of which is sporadic. Three weaknesses of our current approach have been pointed out. First, no central plan for the design and implementation of a comprehensive system has been formulated. A need exists to improve the integration of current efforts to do so, between efforts occurring in different parts of the government and among efforts occurring in the government and those occurring in the private sector. Second, the government is a nonprofit organization. Even if it comes up with the perfect approach, no guarantees exist that the for-profit manufacturing sector will buy in. Incentives will obviously need to be developed and offered. Third, there is a growing fear that the technology will take over and that the "personal touch," so important to healthcare, will be lost.

This latter point was driven home by a nurse who, when asked what she thought about EMR, replied that, "Twenty years ago you took the individual charts and sat down with the others on the case to discuss the patient's condition before visiting the patient's bed. Now, the doctor or nurse goes to a computer to look up lab and test results, in order to determine the plan of care before visiting. Then, after spending several minutes with the patient, the doctor or nurse must hurry back to the computer again to document. Same for medications … check the computer, get meds, give meds, and then return to computer to verify what was given. Laptops help; you can remain in the patient's room while making your entries. But, this approach still limits interaction because you are focused on your entry. There is no touching, no eye contact; you don't want to talk.

"Today's electronic charting actually takes longer than the old paper flowcharts did," she continued, "due largely to the over-regulation of our healthcare system. A hospital has to meet the requirements of the Joint Commission, the Department of Health, CMS, the State Board of Pharmacy–Nursing … and on and on it goes. A great deal of the technology use has been put in place mainly to help us meet these regulations, though we all know that a lot of them contribute little to maintaining, to improving the quality of care delivered, to improving safety. Rather, this additional work just takes more attention away from the patient. When

I think about how much time and money is spent meeting frequently meaningless regulations, how much time is taken away from our supposedly primary responsibility, it makes me sad. And it seems that the more sophisticated our technology grows, the more regulations we have to deal with. The new technology seems to breed them."

Concerning the growing burden of regulations, in the UHS we are designing, there will be one regulatory agency reporting to the National UHS Board of Directors, which reports to the federal Department of Health and Human Services, but is not responsible to it. All sectors needing regulation will be represented in this agency—doctors, nurses, healthcare system administrators, pharmacists, etc. The staff of the regulatory agency will be expected to integrate the regulatory requirements of all these sectors so that one visit by one team can be made to each site rather than multiple visits by multiple teams. Lower levels of the regulatory agency will report to lower level UHS boards of directors.

The National UHS Board of Directors will also be responsible for developing universal regulations, enforcing them through lower level boards of directors, and modifying them on an as-needed basis. A nonpolitical task force composed mainly of technical experts and practitioners in the healthcare sector will be given this responsibility.

U.S. Focus on Individual Pieces of the Healthcare System

Emphasis in the United States up to this point seems to be on increasing the effectiveness of information transfer within individual facilities rather than on increasing it between different parts of the overall healthcare network. Technological innovation aimed at increasing the flow of information within individual facilities has included the development of previously mentioned computers for nursing stations. While these have been available for almost a decade, their cost was initially prohibitive, making the institution of a computerized physician order entry system (CPOE), which is dependent on such technology, impossible. Then, in the late 1990s, as prices dropped, the PDA was introduced to complement the computerized nursing station. Physicians, nurses, and other professionals could now enter and access information immediately from the point-of-care.

Focusing specifically on the ordering and administration of pharmaceuticals, a major weak point in our current healthcare system, according to a 2005 Rand report, an estimated 200,000 adverse drug events could be avoided by converting all U.S. hospitals to electronic order entry.[16]

Ideally, as much as possible of the process of administering medications—from prescription or order entry to administration of the drug—should be done electronically. In fact, the use of a robot is an ideal method for achieving this degree of automation and has been adopted by a growing number of hospital systems. Also, electronically scanned bracelets can help ensure that the right dosage of the right medication is being administered to the right patient at the right time.

All CPOE systems must have the same three basic features to be successful:

1. Ease of use
2. Interoperability
3. Clinical decision support capabilities

Ease of use is a primary indicator for the success of the system. A rapidly expanding range of options is being developed including the real-time syncing of information and physician order entries.

The second indicator of success is the CPOE system's interoperability. The system must be able to access data from various sources including the pharmacy, the laboratory, the business office, and central supply. It should be able to reorder supplies as they are used. Physicians should be able to record services immediately after providing them. The business office should be able to code procedures in real-time.

Though ease of use and interoperability are important, the most important feature of an effective CPOE is its capability to provide clinical decision-making support (CDS). The CPOE will provide physicians with the most up-to-date information available in every treatment situation. Due to the overwhelming and constantly growing quantity of such information, a major challenge is screening. Another challenge is breaking the information down into categories so that every eventuality is addressed.

Once these challenges are solved, CDS can lead the physician and other providers step-by-step through a treatment regime, thus improving patient safety, decreasing length of stay, decreasing costs, and decreasing the number of malpractice claims that arise.[17]

Another piece of the puzzle is what the patient should carry in order to gain access to treatment. In a growing number of more advanced information systems, Smart cards like those found in Germany are being used.

These Smart cards are similar to our current credit cards in that they contain data; in this case, the patient's name, address, emergency contacts, allergies, current medications, recent lab reports, etc. While all this information and more is also stored in the regional data bank, use of the card will facilitate interactions by rapidly providing what is most relevant when, for example, a heavily bleeding patient is brought into a general hospital emergency ward.

To verify identity, cards will be processed the way credit cards are scanned. To provide security in case the card is lost or stolen, a personal identification number (PIN) will be required. A fingerprint audit or a retinal scan could also be used.

An alternative to the Smart card will be a tiny computer chip implanted somewhere on the body that carries the same information. Security, in this case, would obviously not be as much of an issue. In our UHS, both of these alternatives will be optional. The individual citizen will decide whether or not to take advantage of them.

Other strategies of our ideal UIS that will help improve the quality of services delivered by our ideal UHS include:

1. To make immediately available to physicians and other healthcare workers in electronic form patient test results, clinical assessments, evaluations, and management plans.
2. To merge electronic patient records with quality indices and practice guidelines so that care and deviations from "best practices" can be monitored and, if needed, changed or improved.
3. To integrate telemedicine data, including home telemedicine services, into the UIS.
4. To incorporate operative and other procedures into the medical record in real time and with feedback from team members.
5. To include patient Web, telephone, and e-mail communications into the electronic record.

Dealing with Information Needs of the UHS as a Whole

Thus far, as we have said, emphasis in the United States has been on improving the information flow within individual facilities—hospitals, clinics, etc.—and on improving it between these facilities and their satellites.

In our model, however, while this work is of value, it is more important to find ways to link the entire healthcare network together.

Another step in this direction was taken in May of 2001 when the eHealth Initiative was created by 110 healthcare organizations to help address healthcare information challenges. IBM Corporation then approached eHealth Initiative member hospitals, the Centers for Disease Control (CDC), and clinical information technology vendors with a proposal for a joint project, the development of "an interconnected, electronic information infrastructure that operates with open data standards." The project was dubbed the Healthcare Collaborative Network (HCN).

While being easy to use and providing clinical decision support, the HCN, most importantly, allows the transfer of data between different member facilities. This is an important feature because it encourages immediate recognition of abnormal conditions including disease outbreaks as they arise in segments of the population. It also helps identify the value of patient care patterns, including the efficacy of drug therapy.

The benefits of such a system in terms of treatment, research, and, finally, cost, are obvious. IBM estimates that the expense of implementing a HCN for the 110-member healthcare organizations will be approximately $800 million over five years (2003). Considering the Institution of Medicine's claim that a cost of $37.6 billion per year can be attributed to preventable medical errors, and considering the more than $8 trillion that experts predict will be spent on healthcare in the United States over the same five years, $800 million sounds like a pretty good investment.[18]

In relation to our UHS model, however, it is not enough. To be most effective in terms of clinical decision support and ongoing research, the information system must initially span and link the entire national healthcare network, eventually tying into the information systems of other countries.

In order to succeed in this linking process, however, we must first get rid of the competitive environment currently existing in the U.S. healthcare sector. We must also deal with the issue of for-profit insurance companies and the demands they place on information channels. In that all citizens will be allowed to buy private insurance and receive services from that sector as well, private physicians will be allowed access to information from the system on an as-needed basis. Individual clients, however, will be required to release this information. At the same time, insurance companies will not be allowed to use the UIS for the transfer of funds or for market research.

Moving Forward

While we have the beginning of a protocol for our idealized universal information system through the efforts of HL7 and the beginnings of a healthcare information system infrastructure through the efforts of IBM and the Healthcare Collaborative Network, we still have a long way to go on the macro level. Key pieces missing from the U.S. model include:

1. Serious government involvement in developing a UHS and the required information system (UIS). While President Bush started the process and the current administration under President Obama has made the development of universal care and of the necessary information system a priority, we are still in the beginning stages of our effort. This book, hopefully, will help provide a well-thought-out model. The upfront funding for implementation of such a model, however, will have to come mainly from the federal government.

2. Properly secured regional data banks (or "nodes"), linked to each other and to every part of the healthcare network, both administrative and service-oriented.

3. Following Great Britain's lead, linkages between regional data nodes and other social service agencies that impact the health of the population served.

4. An electronic medical record (EMR) for every citizen. Doctors will not have to transfer records when people move. Records will not get lost. People will not have to keep track themselves. Fewer mistakes will be made. Records will be available to healthcare providers anywhere in the country (the world?).

5. Proper safeguards for the information stored in the UIS.

6. Inclusion of drug records in the EMR with automatic checks to guard against the possibility of adverse drug interactions and against patients gaining access to more drugs than is needed.

7. Smart cards carried by patients that store and give access to required EMR patient information. An implanted microchip will be an alternative. The use of either will be optional.

8. A dedicated healthcare Internet portal similar to Sweden's *Guide to Healthcare* that can provide relevant articles and answers to questions, which encourages self-monitoring and self-care, and that

points people in the right direction when they have a problem and facilitates their gaining access to the most appropriate information and treatment.

9. Interactive Web sites will help patients keep track of their individual history concerning cholesterol, weight management, etc. Information will be released from their EMR by a physician. Some of these Web sites will offer tools that patients can use to track and chart their own progress concerning things, such as blood pressure and temperature.

10. Use of Web cams by doctors to contact pharmaceutical representatives for detailed descriptions of products as an alternative to the traditional face-to-face visit and sales pitch. This approach will obviously save the pharmaceutical companies a great deal of money and will cut down on the ability of representatives to offer bribes of any sort to physicians as encouragement to choose their product.

11. A dedicated phone system similar to Great Britain's help line with branches in every state offering a telephone number that community health center staff, their satellites, nursing homes, and public school healthcare facilities can call any time they have a question. Nurses will staff the system and will have access to a wide range of expertise. The nurses can answer the question themselves, they can help search out the most appropriate expert and put the inquirer in touch with that person directly, or they can search out the most appropriate expert, make the query themselves, and relay the requested information to the patient. This system will operate out of the local network's general hospital(s).

12. A second branch of the above phone system that provides the same sort of information and assistance to patients. This system will again be staffed by nurses, but will operate out of the community health center.

13. The use of telemedicine as an alternative to visiting a healthcare facility. This system will be staffed by physician's assistants who have direct access to physicians with different specializations. The telemedicine service will also operate out of the community health center.

14. Electronic home monitoring devices that allow physicians to keep tabs on patients who stay at home.

Implementation

National standards for UIS equipment and processes should be developed during the planning stage of our UHS. A task force of technology and healthcare experts reporting to the National UHS Board of Directors will be responsible for completing this task.

Once these standards are in place and the overall UHS plan is completed, the data "node" in each region will be raised as a first step to implementation. While the technology for these nodes can be purchased from different venders by the regional boards of directors, it must meet the national standards defined, the most important being its ability to communicate effectively with other nodes. Monies will then be distributed to develop the UIS alongside the "pilot" facility network built in each state. Afterward, monies will be distributed to develop the UIS alongside the other networks in each state that model on the pilot. Again, these networks can purchase the technology for their systems from different vendors, so long as it meets the national UHS standards.

RAND has estimated that the full development of a UIS for our UHS will take about fifteen years. We believe that the process will actually be never-ending, due largely to ongoing improvements in technology, but that within five years, the UIS should play a major role in our efforts to provide comprehensive, universal healthcare.

RAND estimates that, even during the startup period, what is in place will create up to $350 billion worth of savings in the inpatient arena and $150 billion in the outpatient arena so that startup costs will be at least partially offset.[19]

REFERENCES

1. Obama's Big Idea: Digital Health Records, David Goldman, CNNMoney.com, January 12, 2009: http://money.cnn.com/2009/01/12/technology/stimulus_health_care (accessed February 15, 2009).
2. *Digital Medicine*, J. Goldsmith, Chicago: Health Administration Press, 2003.
3. Canadian Healthcare Technology: http://www.canhealth.com (accessed February 2004).
4. Calgary Health Region Creates a Leading Edge Chronic Care System, Andy Shaw, *Canadian Healthcare Technology*: http://www.canhealth.com (accessed January 2, 2005).

5. UK Begins $4.7B Electronic Patient Records Project, Bob Brewin, *Bio-IT World*, 2003: http://www.bioitworld.com/new/ (accessed October 21, 2004).

6. Trends in Health Telematics in the European Union, United Kingdom, EHTO Enterprise, SA, 1996: http://www.ehto.org/ht_projects/trends/uk.html (accessed October 15, 2004).

7. A Proposal for Electronic Medical Records in U.S. Primary Care, David Bates, Mark Ebell, Edward Gottlieb, John Zapp, and H.C. Mullins, *The Journal of the American Medical Informatics Association*, January 2003.

8. Britain's Healthcare System Gets a Jumpstart, Micheal Cross, *Healthcare Informatics: International*, 2000: http://www.healthcareinformatics.com/issues/2000/05_00/international.htm (accessed October 16, 2004).

9. Life-Saving Research Missing Out in Health Spending, Richard Wray, *The Guardian Unlimited*, 2004: http://www.guardian.co.uk/business/story/ (accessed October 14, 2004).

10. eHealth in Spain: Current Situation and Major Trends, Jose Luis Monteagudo, Abstract; eHealth 2003—Telematics in Healthcare, National Strategies in Centralised and Federal State Systems, National and International Congress, October 21–23, 2003: http://www.spainhealthcare.com (accessed October 16, 2004).

11. European Physicians, Especially in Sweden, Netherlands and Denmark, Lead U.S. in Use of Electronic Medical Records, *Harris Interactive, Healthcare Research* 2 (16), 2002: http://www.harrisinteractive.com (accessed October 23, 2004).

12. Sweden's Healthcare/IT Advances-Lessons Learned, *ITAC Healthcare Videoconference Simulcast*: http://www.itac.ca/Health/PastEvents/ITAC-SwedensHealthcare.htm (accessed October 23, 2004).

13. *Digital Medicine*, J. Goldsmith, Chicago: Health Administration Press, (2003).

14. To Err Is Human: Building a Safer Health System, *Institute of Medicine*, Washington, D.C.: National Academy Press (1999).

15. A Paperless Healthcare System? A. Sakjeverm, *BusinessWeek*, 2004: http://www. Businessweek. com/technology/content/ jul2004/tc2004077 8164_tc_171.htm (accessed July 7, 2004).

16. Health Information Technology: Can HIT Lower Costs and Improve Quality? *Rand Health* (2005).

17. J. Loyack, personal communication, June 9, 2004.

18. Health Level Seven: Answering the Country's Need for a National Health Information Infrastructure, *IBM*, 2003: http://www.ibm.com/mediumbusiness/resources/whitepapers/whitepaper.jsp?contentId=8564 (accessed February 1, 2004).

19. Health Information Technology: Can HIT Lower Costs and Improve Quality? *Rand Health*, 2005.

6

Profession Education

THE CHALLENGE

Education is critical to building a comprehensive healthcare system. While our system for providing the necessary knowledge and skills has a number of strengths, it also has serious weaknesses. Every healthcare professional must receive a minimum of two years of schooling in order to become proficient in his or her specialty. Some—physicians specifically—must receive six or eight years. Then, there is ongoing education while one is practicing, either required to retain one's license or necessary to stay abreast with changes in the field.

This all costs money. Unfortunately, healthcare education in the United States is more expensive than anywhere else in the world. Students can end up hundreds of thousands of dollars in debt. What they receive for their money is generally high quality, but it is expensive. Research shows that the expense involved frequently deters potential students from studying to be a nurse, a physician, a therapist, or a social worker.

This is a shame because it is becoming increasingly obvious that we do not currently have enough professionals to meet the healthcare needs of our current population, which are continuing to grow as the population expands and ages.

Cost, however, is not the only problem. There are a number of other factors that contribute to this shortage, factors that force us to spend a lot of time and money trying to attract professionals from other countries to fill the gap. One is the lack of training facilities. The Council on Graduate Medical Education has recommended a 15-percent expansion of medical schools.[1]

Another factor is the politicization of the education planning process at the national level, with political views rather than technical expertise too frequently serving as the major consideration when picking those to run the healthcare sector. At least partially as a result of such politics, according to a report by the American College of Physicians, "The United States currently does not have national policies to guide the training, supply, and distribution of healthcare providers. Unlike the United Kingdom and Canada, where single-payer systems give the government the leverage to manipulate the healthcare workforce supply, including control of both training capacity and employment opportunities, comprehensive planning for the health profession in the United States would require coordination among many different funding sources that does not currently exist."[2] Due to politics and "turf" issues, such coordination and planning will be extremely difficult to achieve.

A third "other" factor, which has to do with competition as well as politics, is the lack of standardization throughout our healthcare education sector. School curriculum is not standardized. Placement tests are not standardized. Requirements to practice in different states are not standardized. The United States is the only country in the world where healthcare providers who have been certified to practice in one state are required to pass an "entrance" exam when they move to another part of the country.

When we talk about the staffing needs of a universal healthcare system (UHS), another critical shortage exists. The majority of physicians involved in the system will need to be general practitioners (GPs). Currently, however, 70 percent of our physicians are specialists. The reason for this is quite simple. Specialists make more money, and when you come out of school owing one hundred thousand or two hundred thousand dollars, what you are going to earn is important. In the UHS, of course, the astronomical salaries that some healthcare providers in the United States currently make will be a thing of the past. While life as a provider will certainly be comfortable and probably less hectic, those who want to become overnight millionaires should most likely seek other lines of work.

Again, the American College of Physicians has recommended ways to attract more medical students to general practice that include, "changes in reimbursement policies that (currently) undervalue the contributions of primary care physicians; relief from high levels of student debt; a change to medical education to expose students and residents to positive educational and practice experiences in well-functioning, office-based primary care practices." In other words, pay GPs more, cut the cost of their education, and show them while they are still students that entering the primary care field can lead to a good life.[3]

NECESSARY CHANGES

If we are going to create a successful UHS, a lot of changes need to occur in our healthcare sector. Any student who desires a career and meets the academic requirements should have access to education without incurring a debt that will take years to pay off. Government involvement should be nonpolitical and should focus on facilitation and integration of the system. The healthcare education system should be well integrated with the UHS delivery system, with professionals moving back and forth between the two.

Before we start designing these characteristics into a model, however, let us begin, again, by seeing what other countries with healthcare systems considered superior to ours have put into place.

France

The Ministry of Health and the Ministry of Education control medical education in France jointly. While the entrance exam is extremely competitive, medical school training is funded by the state and, therefore, is almost free, costing no more than a few thousand dollars by the time one's degree is earned. The profession must be popular because we find three doctors for every one thousand habitants, while in Great Britain the ratio is 3:1800, in the United States 3:2700, in Germany 3:3400, and in Italy 3:5900. Also, the number of women doctors in France is growing. More than 40 percent of practicing physicians are women and more than 50 percent of today's medical students are female.[4] The number of students admitted into medical school, the number that can enter any specialization, is limited by ministerial decree. At the same time, however, France is facing a shortage of physicians due to a need for more educational facilities similar to that found in the United States.

Medical training in France includes three phases. Phase one takes two years. During the first year any student with the necessary grade point average can study. In order to continue on through the second year, however, candidates must do well enough on a competitive examination. If they do not pass the exam on the first try, they get one more chance, repeating the first year of study and retaking the exam.

The second phase takes four years during which students receive both theoretical and clinical training. They also receive a monthly stipend to help meet living expenses. Before moving to the third phase, students must pass another examination that tests their theoretical knowledge. They must also complete thirty-six months of hospital internship, becoming familiar with the different specialties.

During the third phase, those training to be general practitioners (GPs) begin a residency that takes two and one-half years. This is followed by a six-month apprenticeship with a licensed GP. Those wishing to specialize must serve four to five years of internship pursuing a diploma in medicine, surgery, psychiatry, biology, or public health. All other subspecializations fall under these five categories. In order to qualify for this training, students must, again, take a competitive examination due to the fact that the number of students accepted yearly into each specialization is limited based on an annual survey of need in the system.

No test is required at the end of their training to receive a license. The degree is all they need to begin practicing.

Curriculum is defined nationally. How it is delivered, however, is decided by the individual schools, many of which are currently encouraging innovative educational techniques, such as problem-based learning, skills-based teaching, and performance-based assessment. By law, all doctors must continue to update their education.[5]

In terms of nursing education, the number of candidates admitted into available programs is again limited by ministerial decree, decisions concerning who is accepted based on completion of a national examination. It takes three years of training to earn a degree in nursing. Those wishing to specialize in surgical, pediatric, or anesthesia must study an additional nine, twelve, and twenty-four months, respectively.

After qualifying to study, pharmaceutical students must complete six years of training. To specialize in hospital pharmacy, they must pass a competitive examination and complete a four-year residency.

Other healthcare professionals (therapists, lab technicians, dieticians, x-ray technicians, etc.) spend from two to four years learning their trade.

Key Features of the French Healthcare Education System

1. Government puts limits on the number of professionals practicing in each field.
2. Competitive exams are taken to decide who is accepted into healthcare training, and who gets to specialize. While anyone with high enough grades can take the first year of medical school training, an exam must be passed to continue on into the second.
3. Education is free.
4. General practitioner students serve a residency followed by an apprenticeship with a licensed GP.
5. Curriculum is defined nationally. How it is taught is left up to the institutions.
6. France is facing a shortage of physicians due partially to a shortage of teaching facilities.

Italy

In Italy, medicine is considered an undergraduate degree that requires six years of study. The first three years provide the foundational sciences including biology, biochemistry, anatomy, physiology, pathophysiology, genetics, and histology. The subjects are presented separately with no effort to integrate them at this level. All courses are followed by examinations that must be passed if one is to proceed.

The second three years address clinical subjects and include lectures on theory. They also include clinical activities under the supervision of tutors. Again, an examination must be passed at the end of each segment in order for the student to continue. The clinical experience is not as important here as it is in other countries, such as in England and Denmark.

At the end of the six years of training, students are required to submit a dissertation in order to receive their degree. The dissertations are usually related to the field in which they intend to specialize. The required research is collected by spending time in the wards under the guidance of a supervisor.

Future physicians studying human medicine (GP) go to school for only the initial six years to win their degree. Those seeking a specialization need to pass an entrance exam for the field and then spend an additional three to five years of study.

Professional fields of study in the Italian healthcare education system include human medicine and surgery, nursing, pharmacy, dentistry, preventative care, midwifery, technical sanitary assistance, and rehabilitation therapy.

Curriculum for the training of nurses is regulated by the national government. The nursing degree requires three years of schooling that include three thousand clinical hours and sixteen hundred theoretical hours. Specializations in nursing that call for additional training include midwifery, elder care nursing, psychiatric nursing, and intensive care nursing.

Education in healthcare professions is, again, largely free. Government each year defines the number of human medicine and specialization slots available. A major current objective of those planning for the Italian system is to produce students qualified to practice in any European country.

Key Features of the Italian Healthcare Education System

1. Initial training requires six years. After that, students can practice as GPs or study another three to five years to specialize.
2. At the end of the initial six years, a dissertation must be submitted. It usually focuses on their desired area of specialization, with the necessary research for it being conducted under supervision in the wards.
3. The number of human medicine (GP) and specialized slots available is defined yearly by the government, with students taking competitive examinations to fill these slots.
4. Curriculum is being shaped to develop the range of expertise necessary for their graduates to practice in any European country.

Denmark

As in Italy, a medical degree requires six years of study. Also, the first three are spent learning the basics, which, for the most part, are the same in both countries. Denmark, however, requires three additional courses that are of interest to our study. These courses are philosophy, psychology, and communication.

Following the first three years, nine weeks are spent in a clinical rotation with a hospital or a general practitioner. During the next three and one-half years of clinical education, subjects are usually taught in individual blocks, which last three to six weeks. Also, as in Italy, a research paper or literary study is required.

The admission process for medical school differs from that of any other country we have studied thus far. Students who have completed their studies at the gymnasium (high school) are allowed to enter any university program they wish including medical school. The weeding out is done during early courses.

The initial six and one-half years of training produces a "basic doctor," who can take a job in a hospital but is not allowed to work independently. In order to practice independently, students must complete graduate work. The graduate work can lead either to a general practitioner (GP) degree or to a specialization. To earn a GP degree, the basic doctor must work in a hospital for another four to five years, focusing on GP issues. During this period, the student must also continue taking courses. In order to specialize, basic doctors must be willing to dedicate between six and eight years to clinical training in a hospital setting.

Currently, one of the things being emphasized in the Danish healthcare education model is team training. It has been pointed out that "ineffective or insufficient communication is a contributing factor in 60 to 80 percent of (adverse) events in medicine." This breakdown occurs when team integration fails.[6]

The team skills focused on during medical school training are leadership, communication, cooperation, and "followership." The key is to get every team member to understand thoroughly what his or her role needs to be in a successful team effort. This is done through simulations using life-sized manikins. Different situations are created. The team must react to them, using whatever technology is required.

Such simulation sessions are divided into three parts. The first is a briefing during which team members are familiarized with the situation they must address including the environment within which they must function. The second part is the actual simulation; and the third is the debriefing during which participants receive feedback from their instructors and from each other. An important tool used during the debriefing is a video account of the event that allows team members to watch themselves in action and to critique their own behavior.

Key Features of the Danish Healthcare Education System

1. Anybody is allowed to enter medical school. The weeding out is done through course examinations.

2. The first six and one-half years of training produce "basic doctors," who are allowed to work in a hospital but cannot practice independently until they have completed the graduate-level work required to become either a general practitioner or a specialist.
3. Emphasis is currently on developing team skills, this being done through simulation exercises and evaluation.

Canada

In Canada, healthcare-related education is not free as it is in other countries we have studied. However, the involved cost is roughly half of that paid for the same training in the United States. The education of physicians in Canada is governed by The Royal College of Physicians and Surgeons. This organization sets standards and disciplines it membership, which includes physicians and surgeons practicing in more than sixty specializations.

The education of physicians in Canada begins at the undergraduate level. After finishing a "normal" undergraduate program, candidates must begin an undergraduate medical education program. Once that is completed, they enter a postgraduate education program at the university level. Curriculum requirements are similar to those of the other countries we have studied. Primary care is an advanced degree along with the other specializations. It is currently more popular in Canada (60 percent of all active physicians) than in the United States (30 percent). This is probably due, at least in part, to the compensation system for physicians, with all fees being set, as we have said, by the provinces.

During the residency, a "return of service" opportunity is made available that covers tuition and board in return for the willingness of a student to provide healthcare-related services to the community. The student is expected to fulfill the obligation while still in school, rather than after graduation. If the service is not delivered, the student is required to make a monthly payment for the service period remaining, plus interest.

The nursing profession is a major concern in Canada. One-third of all current nurses are over 50 years old. Many of the provinces have encouraged the establishment of Career Colleges that offer accelerated learning programs leading to diplomas and certificates in nursing and other healthcare fields. Courses can be taken online at these colleges and programs last between two months and one and one-half years.

A current focus in Canadian healthcare planning is on increasing synergies and dialog throughout the system so that the teaching institutions can learn from each other. In 2007, the Association of Faculties of Medicine in Canada (AFMC) created The Canadian Healthcare Education Commons (CHEC), its mission being to encourage networking between institutions, to encourage the sharing of information and ideas among both faculty and students through the Internet.

Key Features of the Canadian Healthcare Education System

1. A "return for service" program exists for medical students at the resident level that pays for tuition and board in exchange for services rendered to the community while they are still students.
2. A growing number of "career colleges" are being started in the provinces that award diplomas and certificates, while providing enough training to allow students to find lower level jobs as nurses, therapists, etc., in the healthcare field.
3. The CHEC has been formed to encourage improved communication and sharing of expertise and ideas between educational institutions through the Internet.

Japan

The Japanese system is, again, different from most others in key ways. Students, when they enter college, pick their tract, a decision that shapes the rest of their educational career. Those who pick medicine spend six years in their initial training, then two years as interns where they rotate through the different specializations. When they complete the internship segment of their education, students have two choices. One is to pick a specialization and to begin practicing immediately. The other is to spend four more years in their specialization honing their skills.

The rewards for spending four more years are not necessarily financial. Those who do so might attract more patients, or might receive referrals from physicians with patients demonstrating more complex diagnoses. But the payback concerning financial reward is questionable in terms of the additional time spent in school.

Key Features of the Japanese Healthcare Education System

1. Medical training begins as soon as students enter college.
2. Students move immediately to their internship following six years of college with no medical school in between.
3. Students can pick a specialization and begin practicing as soon as they complete their internship, or can spend four more years studying a specialization.

IDEALIZING A UHS HEALTHCARE EDUCATION SYSTEM FOR THE UNITED STATES

Currently, the average amount of debt held by a graduate of medical school in the United States is estimated to be around $140,000 and is rising steadily. In Canada, as we have said, the amount is approximately half that much. In most European countries, it is negligible. Of course, most education in European countries is free, while, especially at the college and graduate levels in the United States, it is increasingly expensive.

We have said that, from a systems perspective, no sector of our society stands alone; all are affected by what is going on in others. In terms of the success of our healthcare system, the education sector especially, a strong influence is exerted on how it is organized and oriented.

The purpose of free education in Europe is to allow every citizen to develop his or her potential to the fullest possible extent. Which university you are admitted to depends on how well you do on a series of highly competitive examinations, the first being taken when you graduate from secondary school. We, of course, have SATs, but they are not nearly as comprehensive as the tests European students take.

Also, there is a movement in the United States to play down SAT scores and depend more on a student's grades when deciding where they will be accepted. *This is a move in exactly the wrong direction.* In Europe students focus on learning during their classes so that they can do well on the end of school examinations. In the United States, students focus too frequently on doing whatever is necessary to get the grade. This can include cheating, bullying the teacher, sabotaging other student's work, getting their parents to bully the teacher, or sucking up.[7]

Education in the United States is increasingly about money. School districts are funded mainly with local taxes, so wealthier areas spend more on the delivery of quality education. I read recently that the Ivy League schools, supposedly among our best academically, are accepting approximately 45 percent of their undergraduates from private schools that cost $40,000 to $50,000 a year to attend. It is said that Ivy League institutions accept the cream of the student population. In reality, it turns out that they might accept the cream, but the cream from a relatively small segment of that population; the defining characteristic of the involved segment being wealth.

Increasing numbers of students cannot attend schools they are qualified academically, or at least intellectually, to attend because they cannot afford the tuition. Even state schools are becoming expensive. An increasing number of students are not going to graduate college because they cannot afford to, because they have to get a job immediately upon completion of college in order to start paying off their debt.

This does not make sense.

As has been said, the countries that are going to do the best, now that the field has been pretty well leveled in terms of access to capital, in terms of technological innovation that can be reverse engineered in a matter of weeks or days, in terms of information that is now globally accessible through the computer, are the countries that most successfully develop and utilize their people's potential. Education is key to such success. It should be free. Access to it should be based on how well one does on competitive examinations, not on how much wealth one's parents possess, and not on how large a contribution one's parents or a friend of the family makes to the alumni fund.

In terms of healthcare training, until our education system catches up, we will have to deal with the constraint that it is not free. Several key issues need to be addressed. One is defining how many physicians and other professionals are actually needed and where they should practice. Right now, as has been said, we are suffering from a shortage. There are not enough physicians, not enough nurses. Just about every field is lacking. A 2004 evaluation of the physician workforce conducted by Richard Cooper, former dean of the Medical College of Wisconsin, and his colleagues suggests, that based on historical trends, the demand for physicians will exceed supply by about 50,000 physicians in 2010, by 150,000 in 2020, and by 200,000 in 2025.[8] Even if these figures do not take into account changes that might occur between now and then, they should be alarming.

This current and projected shortage is and will be due partially, as we have said, to the fact that increasing numbers of potential students cannot afford tuition. A second reason, as we have also said, is the growing shortage of training facilities, of medical schools. A third, rather damning reason for the shortage is that qualified doctors are dropping out, frustrated by the bureaucratic burden imposed by insurance companies, or by the threat of malpractice suits.

Cooper also concluded that, based on the differentiation in earnings, the percentage of physicians who choose to specialize will continue to grow while that of primary care physicians will continue to shrink unless something changes.

These symptoms and others will only grow worse if we do not begin reinventing the system, if we do not begin thinking out of the box.

The Training of Physicians

Starting with the numbers, our local UHS boards of directors will be responsible for submitting on a yearly basis a two-year projection of the staffing needs in every profession at community health centers and their satellites, at specialized clinics, general hospitals, research/teaching/medical hospitals, and nursing homes based on the number of patients served and the types of service delivered. These numbers will be submitted to the state board of directors, compiled, then submitted to the regional board of directors, where they will again be compiled before submission to the National UHS Board of Directors for consideration.

The nonpolitical National UHS Board will be responsible for calculating that year's quota for physicians. It also will be responsible for putting together and administering the set of national exams required of all premed students graduating from college in order to qualify for medical school. Depending on the two-year projections received from lower level UHS boards, the National UHS Board will decide the cut-off point and how many of those taking the test, based on their scores, will be allowed to apply to medical schools.

Students who make the cut off will be allowed to apply to any school they want. If a school received more applications than it has slots to fill, exam scores will be the determining factor as to who is accepted. Those who do not make the cut, as we have said, can try another school. The UHS will be responsible for making sure that enough schools exist to meet the needs of the country. If all of the desired schools are full before a candidate is accepted, that person can wait until the next year and reapply or take the examination again in order to raise his or her score.

A similar arrangement will exist for all other healthcare professions, with the number of slots available based on a two-year projection. Interested students taking a competitive set of exams, and, if qualified, can apply to the school(s) of their choice.

Paying for a Physician's Education

Now it is time to decide how medical education will be paid for by the student, so that after graduation the focus is more on practicing the best possible medicine than on making money, along with digging oneself out of debt.

To solve the problem of rising costs, we propose that students training in healthcare fields are offered *loan forgiveness*. Upon graduation from college, medical school will consist of two more years, as it does now. At the end of the two-year period, students will graduate with the training necessary to become a general practitioner. At that point, all students will take their comprehensive examinations. Those who pass will receive their license to practice. Those who do not pass can study more and take the exam again.

Those seeking loan forgiveness will choose an assignment from a list of openings for GPs in the UHS across the country. The decision as to whether or not a person gets his or her first choice will be decided by the scores earned on the comprehensive examinations and by who else wants that assignment. The new practitioners will then spend two years after graduation in their assignment as a GP. During these two years, they will serve in an apprenticeship role to an experienced GP, functioning as part of that GP's team and receiving a capitation-based salary. This is a takeoff on the centuries-old Chinese tradition of "barefoot doctors." After completing the first year of their apprenticeship, if so desired, the new GPs can change mentors.

Following this period, the physicians will decide whether or not to return to school to specialize. If they decide to remain a GP, they can, at this point choose either to continue working in the UHS or to leave it and begin a private practice or join an already existing one. If professionals do drop out of the UHS, they have the right to rejoin at a later date.

Free market economics will help keep the private practice sector from being flooded. If too many professionals join this sector, there will not be enough work to support everyone. Also, with free treatment available, not everyone will want to pay for the insurance required for treatment in the private sector.

The analysis completed each year by the national or regional UHS boards of directors to determine how many new practitioners will be needed in two years based on the number of patients treated and the types of services delivered will exclude the private sector.

For those who wish to return to school to specialize following their two years as a GP, the choice of who will be accepted will be decided by the scores received on their medical comprehensive examinations. If somebody fails to make the cut-off point for the specialized training most desired, he or she can opt for another specialization where the required score is not as high.

Candidates who pass the exam can apply to any program they wish. If somebody fails to gain entrance into the most desired school, he or she can opt for another one or wait a year and reapply or retake the exam in order to raise his or her score. Once back in school, the same *loan forgiveness* arrangement will be available. After graduating, the specialist will again be required to choose an assignment from a list of openings for specialists in UHS specialized clinics, general hospitals, and research/teaching/medical hospitals across the country in order to pay for the specialization training. Decisions as to who gets what assignment will be based on a national competitive examination. The specialist will work for the two years in his or her assignment as an apprentice to an established specialist in the same field. The new specialist can change mentors after the first year. In most instances, whether serving in a clinic or a hospital, the apprentice will be on salary.

Those who do not enter the loan forgiveness program, those who wish to pay for their education both at the GP and specialist levels, can take the specialization exam immediately upon graduating from medical school. Those who enter the loan forgiveness program but fail to complete their two-year payback apprenticeship(s) will be required to pay for their schooling.

Once accepted into medical school, students will learn what is necessary to become a general practitioner. The curriculum will be standardized across all schools. The National UHS Board of Directors will be responsible for designing it, with input from regional, state, and local boards of directors who, in turn, will gain input from the facilities in their networks. Medical schools will also be asked to contribute as well as the federal governing bodies of the healthcare sector. In France, these bodies would include the Ministry of Finance and the Ministry of Social Affairs. In Italy, the sole body would be the National Health Service. China's Ministry of Public Health plays this role, and, in Japan, it would be the Ministry of Health, Labor, and Welfare.

A long-term plan, already being discussed in Europe, is that curriculum and exams might eventually be standardized not only across Europe, (which they are already working on), but across the world so that physicians, after completing a minimum of additional work aimed mainly at understanding foreign cultures and healthcare-related traditions, can practice anywhere in the world.

Training of Nurses and Therapists

One of the major degree-related issues that should to be addressed by our idealized model concerns nursing in the U.S. healthcare sector where three entry-level positions currently exist based on the amount and type of education required. Those receiving the least overall education are diploma nurses (DN) trained in hospitals. Diploma nurses spend eighteen to twenty-four months in classes and in an apprenticeship role following an experienced nurse as she or he carries out duties, and sometimes being asked to assist.

The strength of this approach is the hands-on clinical experience made possible by the fact that students attend school in a hospital setting. Upon graduation, diploma nurses are well prepared to immediately assume their duties as real-world nurses.

The second level is an associate degree in nursing (ADN). These people spend two to three years enrolled in a community college where they attend classes, take part in laboratory simulations, and travel to a healthcare facility for clinical rotations.

The third level is bachelor's in nursing (BSN). People going for this degree spend four years taking the normal required college or university courses before beginning their major, which is nursing rather than engineering or English.

The confusing part is that in order to earn the right to practice their profession as registered nurses (RNs), graduates of all three of these types of training programs are required to take the same examination. One might think this requirement nonsensical due to the different amounts of education received, but, in fact, all three programs require the same nursing courses. It is the additional ones, or the lack thereof, that differentiates.

So, one might ask, "Why spend four years earning a BSN when one can become a nurse just as easily with a DN?" The answer is that a BSN degree can offer more opportunities in the way of career diversity. A BSN can move from the bedside to pharmaceuticals, to legal, to research, to education, to nursing informatics, to product development, to management, to advanced practitioner, etc. Finally, having earned a BSN gives one a better chance for advancement.

Once they pass the RN exam, students from all three backgrounds start out at the same level of authority and responsibility. After passing the RN exam, those lacking a college degree have the opportunity to continue their education in a BSN program in order to earn this degree. Those who have already earned a bachelor's degree can begin work toward their master's in nursing (MSN).

In reaction to the complicated nature of this approach, efforts are being made in parts of the United States to require all those interested in becoming nurses to go for their BSN degree. In our UHS, due to loan forgiveness, this can be achieved more easily. The major reason people go for their DN in a hospital setting or their ADN at a community college is usually cost. Those two degrees, though possibly not as comprehensive as the BSN, are less expensive. In our UHS-supported education system, because education in healthcare fields will be paid for if one takes advantage of the loan forgiveness opportunity, every future nurse will be expected to earn his/her BSN at a college or university.

The UHS-sponsored BSN degree will combine the classroom and simulation laboratory strengths of the current BSN and ADN degrees with the clinical training strength of the DN degree. It has been estimated that newly graduated nurses take a year to become comfortable in their first job. More emphasis will be placed on clinical training so that these nurses will be better prepared for hands-on responsibilities immediately upon entering the workforce. As the head of a nursing department recently told me, "I believe it is not so much the theory part that is lacking with new nurses, and it is not bedside experience that is missing. I think, rather, that what is missing is the 'putting it all together' experience. We need to find a better way for the new nurses to apply the theory they learn. Unfortunately, that takes time. Great theory or great bedside technique alone makes only average nurses. The two cannot be separated. Great nurses have been given the opportunity to develop both. That is why the BSN as an entry level is the way to go. It allows students the opportunity and the time to gain both."

The clinical training part of the BSN will begin as a mentorship. The student will follow and assist an experienced nurse. Eventually, the trainee will be introduced to the team-building process. The nursing student will begin making rounds and discussing cases as a member of a student team including a medical student, a social worker, a therapist, and perhaps a dietitian. One benefit of introducing the team approach at this point, while its members are still students, is that they will begin to learn the challenges faced by other healthcare disciplines. They will begin to learn how to effectively integrate efforts and how to make use of each other's expertise. The group's efforts will be monitored and facilitated by a hospital staff member in combination with university faculty members.

All therapists, as now, will be required to earn graduate degrees in order to practice. The degrees will be for physical, occupational, and expressive therapy as well as recreational art, music, and dance therapy. The education/training of somebody interested in earning a degree in one of these fields can begin in a community college or in a university. Once students complete their initial four years of education/training, they can work as an assistant to a licensed therapist, but cannot practice on their own. In order to do this, they must earn their master's degree. All therapists will be eligible for the loan forgiveness program.

The healthcare network, in conjunction with the education community, will provide continuing education for all types of professionals.

The nurses and therapists who take advantage of loan forgiveness, like physicians, will be required to spend payback time in a placement assigned by the UHS. RNs can continue on for their master's in a specialized field after two years of practice. They will again be eligible for the loan forgiveness program, though, they must be willing to accept another assignment from the local UHS Board of Directors as payment.

New Course Requirements

Once students are enrolled in a school offering their health-related field, be it medicine, nursing, therapy, social work, etc., they will be required to take one course in economics/business skills. Through this course, they will become familiar with how the healthcare system is financed, how it fits into the rest of the economy, and the basic skills needed to run a business—financing, accounting, marketing, management, planning, etc.

Though most students will eventually be working in the UHS rather than the private sector, thus making many of the business skills taught unnecessary, it is important that the students understand how the system works so that they can suggest improvement through their local boards of directors, and understand the changes that are occurring.

For those who eventually decide to go into private practice, what is learned in this course will, obviously, be of great importance, with many of the new physicians, at some point in their career, returning to school to receive their MBA. Also, those who become administrators in the UHS will, at some point, be required to earn their MBA or a master's-level degree in healthcare management.

A course in preventative healthcare will also be required. This course will include communication skills that will stress the development of the ability to understand the social customs of different cultures. In that this emphasis will be on prevention more so than treatment in our UHS, all future providers will function as teachers when tending to patients. To increase their effectiveness, they will survey, in this course, topics including diet, exercise, mental health, self-examinations, yoga, meditation, prevention education, and so forth.

During the course, students will also explore how best way to deliver education to different personality types in different situations. We have all run into healthcare providers who lacked important social skills. We have all run into healthcare providers who were impatient, condescending, and/or rude. On the other hand, providers have all run into patients who were afraid, argumentative, demanding, or uninterested. This course will address both sides of the coin. Students will learn the basics of a "good bedside manner." They will also learn how to deal with a range of patients, some very difficult, possibly using role-playing as a vehicle. Videos will be created so that students can watch themselves in action and critique their own performance.

This training will be valuable to physicians in particular because, with our new UHS reward system based on capitation and on the number of people that enroll each year rather than on the number of treatments delivered, emphasis will switch from efficiency, from wasting as little time as possible while diagnosing and tending to patients, to developing a thorough understanding of potential ailment producers that can be remedied or avoided in the future.

The ability to communicate and to be empathic needs to be instilled in medical students and must continue to be enhanced at least through their early careers. While this "let's get to know you" approach encouraged by our UHS model takes more time, it is time well spent, both in terms of treating the patient properly and in terms of the physician and the rest of his or her team benefiting financially by keeping patients healthy.

A third topic addressed in this class, as we have said, will be cultural diversity. Students will learn what is acceptable and unacceptable in other cultures concerning customs and religion. They will also become familiar with the different beliefs found in those cultures concerning medical treatment. For example, in some areas of Africa, when a family member goes to the hospital, all the others tag along and sleep in the room, leaving during the day to go to work or do other things, but returning in the evening, usually with food for the patient.

These two courses, and as many others as is feasible, will be taught not just to classes containing one type of professional, but to classes containing a mix that might include future physicians or nurse practitioners, physician's assistants, nurses, social workers, dieticians, therapists, and psychologists. Because service delivery in the UHS community health centers will be based on a team approach, the development of appropriate interactions and interdependencies among future team members should begin in the classroom. As in Denmark, simulations will be used, complete with an upfront briefing spelling out the situation and environment; the simulation itself that will frequently include an entire family, and the debriefing.

Manikins will serve as patients or clients, but also live actors can take part making the situation more realistic and dynamic. The entire exercise will be videotaped so that team members can watch themselves in action.

Obviously, the organizing of such integrated classes will necessitate a joint planning effort by the professional training departments involved.

Finally, a type of "capstone" course, usually the last one taken as a means of bringing the disciplines together, will provide the teams with a family or families to work with under the supervision of university professors and healthcare professionals. For example, the Jones family has four children. One of the children is on drugs, another has diabetes. Everybody in the family is overweight, with the mother very much so. The father has a job, but is in danger of losing it because he drinks heavily. The suspicion is that he has abused his wife.

How do you deal with this family, all members of which are constantly coming to the community health center for treatment, frequently when nothing is wrong; the son and mother using up their allowance by the middle of the year and being paid for out of the catastrophic fund? The temptation might be to decide they are hopeless and to spend as little time as possible with them. But the team's bonus is based on the amount of money family members *don't* spend out of their allowance. So, it is to the team's benefit to try and turn them in a healthier direction.

The physician or physician's assistant will obviously deal with the diabetes. But because diet affects the ailment, the nutritionist/dietician will need to become involved, also attempting to address the overweight issue. In terms of the father's alcoholism and job situation, the social worker will need to spend time with him, investigating the suspected wife abuse as well, maybe bringing in the psychologist or even a clinic-based psychiatrist when it is discovered that the father is severely depressed and might need medication. The physical therapist will try to get the mother to begin walking and eventually working out at the local fitness center.

And how do all these pieces fit together? How do they complement each other? The student team members would have to figure that out.

The question of who should be the team leader will arise during team training sessions and later when team members are actually working in a community health center. Physicians have traditionally taken this role, and are the ones to give the orders. In certain situations, like the operating room, there indeed needs to be one unquestioned leader. However, that role will be somewhat softened during the normal routine of the community health center. Each professional will bring his or her expertise to the table and will take the lead when appropriate.

For example, with the Jones family, when asked about her diet by the physician, the mother lies and says that she eats mainly salads and that her obesity and the fact that it is growing steadily worse is strictly the result of heredity. However, during the weekly team conference, when the case of this mother and family is brought up, the social worker, who has spent time in the home, might point out that all she saw lying around were empty doughnut boxes and that when she looked in the refrigerator there was nothing green, only bottles and cans of soda.

Obviously, while the medication administered by the GP is important, the work done by the social worker in the home is equally important, and the work done in the future by the nutritionist and the physical therapist will be important.

Regardless of the program of study pursued, students will complete clinical rotations in community health centers, specialized clinics, general hospitals, teaching/research/medical hospitals, and nursing homes. This will be done to provide them with real-world experience. It will be done to encourage the development of effective patient interaction and clinical skills. It will be done to help them understand the network, its parts, and how the parts fit together.

In each of these settings the student will be assigned a mentor. In each setting the student will function, hopefully, as part of a team, or as an assistant to a team member. This will again help to reinforce the team mentality.

The grading system in all healthcare-related training programs will be pass/fail, the emphasis being on learning through cooperation rather than on competing for the highest possible grade. The competition will come later during the placement examination period following graduation.[9]

Education for the healthcare professionals in the ideal UHS will not end after attaining a degree. It will not end after finding a placement in the healthcare community. Practitioners in all fields must earn continuing education credits/units. These can be achieved through specific seminars/conferences and classes that may be offered at hospitals, colleges/universities, or other locations.

UHS staff will be allowed to attend individual university classes, if there is room, to gain their yearly required continuing education credits. These credits can be organized to build toward an advanced degree in the same field or toward a degree in another field of healthcare expertise. All continuing education credits earned while one is employed by the UHS will be free.

A close association will exist between the college/university(s) that are situated within the boundaries of the local healthcare network, the Local UHS Board of Directors planning for that network, and the healthcare facilities located within it. The dean of the local medical school or the head of the department offering healthcare-related courses will be a member of the Local UHS Board of Directors. Faculty from the medical school, those teaching healthcare courses, will be encouraged to sit on the advisory committees of local community health centers and specialized clinics.

A member of the Local UHS Board of Directors will be a member of the university's decision-making body. Professional staff from the various facilities will function as guest speakers to related university departments. If qualified, if they want to, these people might also teach as adjunct professors.

REFERENCES

1. Reforming Dysfunctional Payment Policies, underdraft by the Medical Services Committee of the American College of Physicians, Philadelphia, 2009.
2. *Creating a New National Workforce for Internal Medicine*, position paper, American College of Physicians, Philadelphia, 2006.
3. *Creating a New, National Workforce for Internal Medicine*, 2006.
4. Country Report: Medical Education in France, *Medical Education*, 41 (3), March 2007.
5. France's Model Healthcare System, Paul Dutton, *The Boston Globe*, August 11, 2007.
6. Implementation of Team Training in Medical Education in Denmark, H.T. Ostergaard, D. Ostergaard, A. Lippert, *Quality of Health Care*, 13 (Suppl. 1), 2004.
7. "Yes, Tests Still Rule," William F. Roth, *American School Board Journal*, 192 (5): May 2005, 57–58.
8. Medical Schools and Their Applicants: An Analysis, Richard Cooper, M.D., *Medical Affairs*, 22 (4), 2003.
9. Bringing Pass/Fail to Preclinical Curricula, *American Medical Student Association*, 2003: http://www.amsa.org/meded/passfail.cfm (accessed November 15, 2003).

7

Dealing with Malpractice

THE CHALLENGE

Even though our new model for healthcare in the United States will allow many improvements in terms of delivery, malpractice is not going to disappear. Doctors and other healthcare providers will continue to make mistakes, mostly unintentional, but still mistakes that can inhibit the ability of victims to lead a normal life or to earn a living; mistakes that cause a great deal of physical pain or mental anguish. It is estimated that despite our continual advances, medical mishaps remain the eighth leading cause of death in the United States, ahead of such things as automobile accidents and AIDs. Such mishaps and their consequences must be addressed.[1] Victims of medical malpractice should have the right to seek and receive restitution.

At the same time our current approach to dealing with such misfortunes costs the healthcare system quite a bit, payment being made to insurance companies for the initial insurance, to lawyers for pleading the cases, to expert witnesses who testify, and, eventually, to the victim. The question is: Does a less expensive way exist that allows us to deal with this issue in a fair manner? We think so, but first let us explore the malpractice "mess" in more detail.

Medical malpractice can be defined as professional negligence occurring through an act or omission by a healthcare provider; that is, the care that is given deviates from accepted standards of practice in the medical community and causes injury to the patient.

The need in a malpractice claim is for the patient to prove that the physician or another healthcare practitioner has not met one of these standards—that the physician, for example, has cut off the wrong leg or left a surgical instrument inside the patient. In order to do this, the patient finds a lawyer who specializes in malpractice cases.

Because the average length of such a case is five years, legal expenses can run high. At the same time, many of the involved lawyers work on a "contingency fee." There is no upfront payment; rather, the lawyer takes a percentage of the final award, typically one-third, sometimes 50 percent or more.[2] Expert witnesses are also frequently used. They are qualified medical experts brought in to help prove that the defendant deviated from an accepted medical standard. These witnesses are expensive as well.

At the end, therefore, when everything is finally added up, it is estimated that for every dollar spent on victim compensation more than 50 percent goes to administrative expenses including lawyers, expert witnesses, and the courts.[3]

For all of the above reasons, lawyers aim for a high settlement, which now averages above $1 million when a jury is involved. Most healthcare professionals, or course, if convicted, cannot personally afford to pay such a penalty from their own assets. Therefore, they are forced to buy malpractice insurance, which again brings private, profit-driven insurance companies into the game.

Malpractice insurance premiums continue to go up, especially for internists, surgeons, and obstetricians, jumping 20 to 25 percent in the year 2002 alone.[4] This is partially because jury awards have been know to jump as much as 40 percent in one year.[5] But, while insurance companies try to blame this unreasonable rise on lawyers and patients seeking lucrative settlements, a strong argument is being made that the major cause is insurance companies wanting to increase their profit margin. Proof of this argument is that while malpractice payments decreased by 8.2 percent between 2001 and 2002, physicians' premiums did not decrease at all. In fact, they continued to climb. By the middle of this decade, obstetricians with a practice in the state of Florida were frequently paying over $200,000 for malpractice insurance. While the cost for similar insurance was lower in other states, it was and still is in the tens of thousands of dollars.[6]

OUTSIDE ASSISTANCE

Attempts are currently being made to protect healthcare providers from the cost of malpractice insurance. One approach has been for professional associations to form their own insurance companies in order to keep the cost down. More than half of our physicians currently buy their insurance from such programs.[7] An advantage of this arrangement is that most of the association-owned companies are nonprofit. They must still deal, however, with the exorbitant cost of settlements. Thus, the premiums required can still be high.

Another approach is for states to actually provide the necessary insurance for healthcare practitioners. For-profit companies, when forced by market pressures or regulations to cap or to lower their premium rates, can simply stop providing malpractice insurance, leaving practitioners vulnerable to disastrous lawsuits. The states have stepped in to provide an affordable alternative, being careful, up to this point, not to severely under-price free market competitors. West Virginia, for example, requires that the price of state-sponsored insurance be higher than that offered by private firms. Actually, then, while this strategy assures the availability of coverage for practitioners, it does little to assist those for whom cost is the major concern.

A third tactic is for some level of government to subsidize a portion of private malpractice insurance for providers. Such subsidies can remain in place until the price of premiums drop to an acceptable level. They can be used to help physicians whose premiums are highest, and they can act as an incentive to encourage healthcare providers to take jobs in geographical areas that are underserved.

But, because no pressure is being applied in this situation, the price of private insurance premiums obviously is not going to drop. Why should the price drop when the purpose of the game is to make as much profit as possible? Instead of finding ways to force the price of malpractice insurance down, therefore, the government is using taxpayer dollars to support these prices and to protect profits in the insurance industry.

If our objective is to develop the most cost-effective UHS healthcare system possible, this approach does not make sense, at least in the long term.

A fourth alternative exists for those healthcare providers working for a city, county, or state, usually in a public hospital, a public clinic, or in a state university hospital system. In this instance, when a claim is made against a provider, it is shifted to the state. The state becomes responsible for mounting the defense and for paying the reward. The threat is that the state with all its wealth now becomes the target for lawsuits. The threat is that jury-defined awards might run higher when the state is the defendant.

A fifth strategy has been for states, rather than subsidizing healthcare providers' premiums, to pay a portion of injury rewards after they reach a certain level, thus relieving healthcare providers of part of the debt burden. The funding for this program comes from a surcharge assessed against those providers who join the program. In some states, joining is voluntary; in some states it is required. The problem here, of course, is that the approach again does nothing to hold down premiums paid for private malpractice insurance, while, at the same time, adding a second premium that the provider must pay.

HOLDING DOWN THE SIZE OF REWARDS

Coming from an entirely different perspective, rather than seeking outside assistance from professional organizations, from state or federal government in paying for malpractice insurance, rather than government paying a portion of the reward, attempts are being made to diminish the size of decisions. This approach involves tort reforms. The purpose of tort reforms is to limit the size of injury rewards. In turn, this will help reduce the cost of coverage.

One of the proposed ways of doing this is to take into account the fact that a plaintiff is, at the same time, receiving payment from sources other than the defendant's malpractice policy, that the plaintiff is receiving payment from, say, a health insurance policy, or from disability.

Another way of accomplishing this is to place a cap on the amount that can be collected by the plaintiff. Two types of damages are involved in malpractice suits. The first is "economic damages." This has to do with the amount the victim will lose due to injury, lost work time, medical expenses, etc. The second is "noneconomic damages" including both physical and psychological suffering and loss of the ability to interact socially. It is estimated that approximately one-third of all rewards goes toward "noneconomic damages." In some cases, "punitive damages" are also allowed, an amount being awarded to punish the involved physician for behaving in a reckless manner.

Economic damages are relatively easy to define because they are quantifiable. One simply has to add up the numbers. The definition of non-quantifiable, noneconomic damages, however, is usually an exercise in subjectivity. This is the area where a growing majority of healthcare providers want to apply a cap. The amount of such a cap frequently discussed is $250,000. Lawyers, of course, argue strongly against any limit, especially one so low in terms of what has been awarded during the past few years. The lawyers argue that a cap would cause their client to be punished and to be treated unfairly.

"Sovereign immunity caps" exist for the previously mentioned healthcare providers who work for public hospitals or in other public programs where malpractice claims are shifted to the state. These caps are usually much lower than the ones found in the private sector.

Another approach to limiting court-delivered rewards to the injured is to eliminate "joint and several liability." This is a legal statute that makes each healthcare provider involved potentially liable for the total amount of the reward sought by the victim if the plaintiff's lawyer decides to focus on one person rather than choosing to focus on what portion of the damage for which each provider should potentially bear responsibility. Obviously, this is not fair in that the person with the most coverage can be and frequently is made to pay.

Concerning contingency fees, a way to reduce the current emphasis on profit that drives malpractice rewards up is for states to cap the amount lawyers handling malpractice suits can earn. As we have said, rather than charging a set amount, they take a percentage of the reward. Lawyers are against such a change, of course. Their argument is that without such an arrangement the client will not be able to find representation and will end up with nothing. Despite the very real possibility of this happening, many states have defined limits.

Pretrial screenings are also used to decide the merit of each case in an attempt to weed out those that shouldn't be heard, those that are "frivolous," in order to save court costs and to save the money spent on legal representation. The panel that does the screening is generally composed of a lawyer, a physician, and a public advocate. In some states, the panel's decisions are binding. In some states, they may be submitted only as recommendations.

Finally, in order to hold down the cost of rewards, a statute of limitations can be imposed to stop potential plaintiffs from filing suits after a certain amount of time has passed. The argument against this, of course, is that damage resulting, for example, from an operation might not show up for years.

ELIMINATING THE NEED FOR TRIALS

Coming from a third perspective, rather than providing outside assistance in covering the cost of malpractice insurance or in paying rewards, rather than finding ways to hold down the cost of decisions, efforts can be made to deal with the situation, to make a financial judgment before it reaches the courts. Some states have done this by establishing "no fault liability funds." Each fund addresses one type of injury, usually having to do with birth trauma. The claim is presented to a panel of physicians that decides whether or not it is legitimate, whether or not it meets predefined criteria. If it is legitimate, if it does meet predefined criteria, the victim receives lifetime benefits, the compensation being limited to economic loss including salary, medical, and rehabilitation expenses.

Arbitration is also an alternative to going to trial and also involves a panel. But this time the panel includes an attorney, a healthcare provider, and a public advocate. The plaintiff's decision to use arbitration is voluntary. The panel's decision is binding and reward payments are usually lower. However, the plaintiff saves time, the cost of a lawyer, and the cost of expert witnesses.

Another approach is the "early offer and rapid recovery" alternative. If this approach is adopted, the provider, an individual or organization against whom a claim is filed, has 120 days to offer an ongoing, no-fault-type payment based on projected economic loss suffered by the patient. If the offer is accepted, any possibility of collecting for non-economic loss is lost. A reason for turning it down would be the plaintiff's belief that the healthcare practitioner's offense was intentional. In order to prove this, however, the plaintiff will need the services of a lawyer, who will cost money. Also, an award, if won in court, will not be available for several years, probably making the "early offer and rapid recovery" alternative more attractive.

HOW MALPRACTICE IS HANDLED IN OTHER COUNTRIES

And there we have it, many different ways of protecting practitioners from the cost of malpractice insurance and from legal judgments concerning malpractice, all of which are being used by institutions in the healthcare domain, all of which have weaknesses. The high degree of individualism found in our malpractice insurance "mess" again demonstrates the confusion found in the U.S. healthcare realm. Ours is the only developed country that has not yet put together one unified system for sensibly limiting the cost of malpractice insurance and to keep the cost of suits under control. So, now it is time to look at what other countries with healthcare systems, supposedly superior to ours, have in place, and possibly to learn from their models.

Sweden

When we talk about Sweden's approach to malpractice, we are also talking about Norway's, Denmark's, and Finland's. We may as well call this approach the Scandinavian Model, noting that it seems to be gaining popularity in other parts of the world as well, including New Zealand. The Swedish model is built around no-fault. Rather than filing a claim, those who have been injured fill out a form that is made available by all hospitals and clinics. The form is straightforward. On it the claimant describes what has been done to him or her that should be construed as malpractice. All completed forms are then channeled to a government-appointed review board for judgment. The board includes three representatives from the healthcare unions that practitioners belong to and five other elected members.

While approximately three patients in Sweden file a malpractice claim for every one that files a claim in the United States, nearly 50 percent of these claims are eliminated as frivolous or as unworthy of the review board's attention. Of those that are accepted for review, 40 percent receive compensation. The level of noneconomic payments awarded is set according to a table. These levels are not subject to appeal. The maximum amount anybody can receive for the combination of economic and noneconomic damages is around $1 million, the award being paid from a government compensation fund that is supported by tax revenues. The average payout, however, is approximately $10,000.[9]

Appeals are possible. An arbitration board exists to handle them. The entire appeal process can, again, be handled through the mail. If the patient is still not satisfied, he/she can hire a lawyer and take the case to court, though payments awarded by the courts are generally lower than those paid though the compensation fund.

As a result of this no-fault setup, malpractice insurance is obviously not as important in Sweden as it is in the United States. Healthcare providers in Sweden are, however, required to carry a relatively small amount of insurance purchased from a private insurance company to cover situations where the plaintiff is not satisfied with the review board award or with the award gained through an appeal to the arbitration board, and takes the case to court.

In terms of disciplining healthcare providers for errors considered unacceptable in terms of predefined standards, a medical responsibility board has been created to investigate the circumstances behind all claims that are accepted by the review board. It is estimated that approximately 20 percent of all claims reviewed by the medical responsibility board result in physicians receiving a warning or admonition that becomes part of their record. It is estimated that in 1 percent of the cases the physician's license is revoked.

Key Features of the Swedish Malpractice Insurance and Compensation System

1. The entire system is based on no-fault. The level of noneconomic rewards is defined by a schedule. The maximum combination of economic and noneconomic awards cannot exceed $1 million, the average award being approximately $10,000.
2. All reward payments come from a compensation fund supported by tax revenues.
3. Claims are made by filling out a form available at all treatment facilities. The form is then mailed to a review board that makes decisions concerning compensation.
4. Unsatisfactory review board decisions can be appealed to the arbitration board.
5. Unsatisfactory arbitration boards decisions can be carried to the courts, though, at this point, a lawyer must be retained and compensated.
6. A medical responsibility board looks into the circumstances of every case brought before the review boards. It decides if the involved

healthcare provider deserves punishment. If punishment is merited, the medical responsibility board defines its nature and delivers it.

7. Healthcare providers are required to carry a relatively small amount of private insurance to cover claims taken to the courts.

France

Not too long ago, France's malpractice system resembled that of the United States. Healthcare practitioners had to buy insurance from private firms. Patients desiring to file a complaint found a lawyer and went to court. There were no caps on rewards, but it was more difficult for the plaintiff to win because medical standards were not as high as they are today. Thus, the plaintiff had a harder time proving fault. No way existed of settling without going to court. Also, no way existed to appeal the court's ruling.

Now France's approach to malpractice more closely resembles that of Sweden and the other Scandinavian countries, this shift being caused at least partially by the rising cost of premiums. France's healthcare system has an approach to malpractice that mixes fault and no-fault. Victims register their claims with a government-appointed regional commission that decides if the case should be heard. If the case is heard and is judged no-fault, a set amount is awarded. If there exists a possibility of fault, it is the physician's responsibility to prove no medical error was involved. If the physician is found to be at fault, the commission decides how much the victim should be awarded. If a victim is not satisfied with the compensation offered, that person has the right to refuse it, to hire a lawyer, and to take the case to court.

The money used to pay rewards comes from a national compensation fund that is supported, unlike Sweden's compensation fund, mainly by insurance premiums paid by healthcare providers. Providers who are affiliated with UHS hospitals and clinics have their premiums for government-sponsored insurance paid for by their organization. Providers who opt for an individual practice in the UHS pay their own premiums; but they must purchase the same government-sponsored insurance. The price of the UHS malpractice premium is set by the government and does not fluctuate according to the free market. When the amount of insurance premium revenues received from UHS providers do not cover payouts from the fund, general tax revenues are added to the pot.

Those who opt to work in the French private sector must purchase their insurance from private companies. Malpractice cases that arise in the private sector do not go to the regional commission, but, rather, they go immediately to the courts. Rewards are paid by the healthcare provider's private insurance policy.

Again, because it is a much simpler process, because it is cost-free and takes less time, the number of malpractice claims brought by patients in France (against the UHS) is much higher than in the United States. At the same time, however, the level of rewards is much lower.

Key Features of the French Malpractice Insurance and Compensation System

1. The system is a mix of fault and no-fault.
2. Compensation levels for no-fault decisions are set.
3. A regional commission hears cases and makes decisions.
4. Rewards come from a national compensation fund that is supported mainly by the premiums paid by healthcare workers for government-sponsored insurance. Any shortfall in the fund is covered by general tax revenues.
5. Those injured, if not satisfied with their UHS reward, can get a lawyer and take their case to court.
6. Private practitioners must buy malpractice insurance from a private firm. If a claim is filed against a private practitioner, it goes directly to the courts.

Great Britain

In the United Kingdom, as in France, physicians can choose to work either in the public or private sector. The 90 percent who choose the public sector are insured by and have their insurance paid for by the National Health Service that is supported by tax-based government revenues. In the private sector, healthcare providers must purchase their own insurance. Public sector doctors cannot be held personally liable for injury. Rather, the National Health Service is the defendant. Private sector doctors are sued as individuals. This helps explain why the public sector is more attractive.

There is no panel or commission to decide public sector cases out of court. All cases, both public and private sector, go to court. Here, the plaintiff is at greater risk of financial loss than in other countries we have studied. Malpractice lawyers do not work on contingency fees as in the United States, but demand payment, win or lose. Also, a "loser pays" approach exists. If the plaintiff loses in the public sector, that person must pay not only his or her own legal fees, but those of the National Health Service as well. In the private sector, the plaintiff who loses must pay those fees of the physician sued.

The United Kingdom is reported to be moving toward the "Scandinavian Model" in the areas of ophthalmology and OB/GYN, developing a schedule of payouts. A new twist in the OB/GYN area is that physicians are required to write a letter of apology when an error occurs, explaining what happened to the injured patient and why.[10]

As a result of this approach to malpractice, less than half the number of claims per capita filed in the United States are filed in the United Kingdom. The average payout is close to $100,000.

Key Features of the British Malpractice Insurance and Compensation System

1. Healthcare providers who choose to work in the public sector have their malpractice insurance paid for by the National Health Service, which is funded by tax revenues.
2. All cases, both public and private sector, go to court where a "loser pays" approach is used.
3. The National Health Service rather than the physician is the defendant in public sector cases.
4. Malpractice lawyers do not work on a contingency fee basis, thus the plaintiff must pay for services win or lose.
5. The United Kingdom is moving toward the "Scandinavian Model" in the areas of ophthalmology and OB/GYN with the additional requirement that offending OB/GYN physicians must write a letter of apology to patients explaining what happened.

Japan

The Japanese Medical Association (JMA) provides malpractice insurance for approximately 45 percent of Japan's 250,000 physicians. Premiums are relatively low compared to those of the other countries we have studied—between $450 and $500 annually. This is due in large part to the low number of claims registered, less than 1 per 100 physicians, and to the fact that though the amount paid through awards is growing, it remains close to $100,000.[11]

The JMA offers a nonbinding, out-of-court review of claims that saves time and money, taking just a few months, requiring no lawyer and no court fees. The weakness of this approach, of course, is that physicians are being required to pass judgment on physicians. Due to the culture of respect found in Japan, one might suspect that this arrangement puts the plaintiff at a serious disadvantage. Also, because the JMA provides malpractice insurance, it is responsible for making the payment when judgments favor the plaintiff.

As in most of the other countries studied, plaintiffs have access to the traditional court system with their case if they can afford a lawyer and are willing to wait approximately three years for a verdict.

Key Features of the Japanese Malpractice Insurance and Compensation System

1. The Japanese Medical Association provides insurance for nearly half of the country's physicians at a price of between $450 and $500.
2. The Japanese Medical Association reviews claims and decides settlements for free.
3. If they can afford the expense in terms of both time and money, Japanese plaintiffs who do not accept the decision of the Medical Association still have access to courts.

Similarities in the Countries Studied

Similarities are obvious concerning the treatment of malpractice in most of the countries with healthcare systems considered more comprehensive than ours. The first of these similarities is that all of these countries have one approach to controlling the price of malpractice insurance and malpractice cases, rather than multiple approaches. Either the public sector handles these issues, or a joint public sector/private sector system exists, the responsibilities of the two sectors segregated and clearly defined.

The second similarity is that providers receive their insurance free from the government or purchase it from a government or professional organization that is not profit-driven. The price of premiums is adjusted solely to cover costs. Approximately half the physicians in the United States have this same opportunity, though their premiums are uniformly higher.

The third similarity is that some form of an expert panel has been established to review cases and makes judgments. The panel's efforts are free in order to save on court cost and to save time. In Japan, this panel is composed totally of physicians, which most likely is a mistake in that as in most cultures the natural inclination of panel members would be to favor one of their own rather than the plaintiff.

Such an alternative does not exist only in Britain and Italy (in the countries studied). All cases in these two nations must go to court. While Britain is moving toward the Scandinavian Model of a predetermined schedule of payments for noneconomic rewards, Italy continues to struggle with the same problems plaguing the United States. Because all cases go to court and no caps have been established, rewards tend to run higher, insurance premiums are rising steadily, insurance companies are backing away from involvement, and the practice of defensive medicine is increasing, with doctors focusing more on documentation and other defensive measures than on treating their patients properly.

The fourth similarity is that in all countries with review panels, the plaintiffs, if not satisfied with their reward, can hire a lawyer and take their case to court. Most of the lawyers work on a contingency fee, as in the United States. In Britain, however, they do not, thus putting the client at greater risk of financial loss.

The fifth similarity is that most of these countries offer either a no-fault system or a mixture of no-fault and fault.

The sixth similarity is that most of the countries studied have established caps or a schedule of the payments that are to be rewarded to victims for a range of injuries in both the economic and the noneconomic portion of suits.

Back to the U.S.

The best way to protect healthcare providers from the cost of malpractice insurance and suits, of course, is to eliminate or at least to limit the need for insurance by getting rid of errors. While the concept of "zero defects" in the industrial world is misguided (the concept should be continuous improvement; workers should be encouraged to learn from their mistakes), the concept of "no errors" in the field of healthcare where even the smallest mistake might put a life at risk makes complete sense.

The first thing we need in order to cut down on the number of suit-producing errors in healthcare is a universal set of standards and guidelines by which to judge the activities of professionals. But, once again, the standards/guidelines "mess" in our healthcare system is difficult to comprehend. We have Joint Commission standards that focus on record keeping and housekeeping. We have the Office of Minority Health Standards. We have the Health Skill Standards Project. We have the Standards for Healthcare Advocacy in Healthy People 2020 Project.

In terms of organizing and making standards and guidelines available to practitioners and the public, we have the Healthcare Information Technology Standards Panel and The Healthcare Standards Landscape Project, which, in turn, work with the ANSE, the AHRO, the CHS, the NAHIT, the ADA, the IEEE-1073, the HL7, and the NCPDP. And this is just part of what exists at the national level. The state level is a whole new ballgame.

There are two ways of dealing with this mess. The first is to try to develop a channel through which one can figure out which of these sources is most relevant and through which one can access them. This is what the Healthcare Standards Landscape Project is trying to do through the Internet. The second way is to condense as many of these different sources as possible into one vehicle that is made easily available to all.

Our model for dealing with malpractice will be built around the second approach. We will begin by addressing the challenge of establishing a set of national standards and identifying a set of universally accepted best practices so that it is easier to determine if malpractice has occurred. It will be impossible, of course, to cover every situation, but such an effort will at least provide a solid foundation on which to build as well as an easily accessible source of information for both healthcare practitioners and the public.

The National UHS Board of Directors will finance this effort and assemble the necessary expertise. The process will, of course, be on-going as healthcare theory and technology continues to evolve. The standard/best practices defined will be used as a springboard for all decisions made in malpractice cases. The group of experts will be independent. It will not report to politicians, but to the National UHS Board of Directors.

Our model will also allow healthcare providers in the UHS to purchase malpractice insurance from the government through the National UHS Department of Healthcare Administration. Premium rates will be set, as in France, not to generate profit, but to assure that providers have comprehensive protection at the least possible cost while still paying all expenses of the system including rewards to plaintiffs.

Healthcare professionals in the private sector will purchase their own insurance from for-profit companies. Again, these companies will be allowed to adjust their rates with profit as the main objective, but will now have real competition, not from each other so much as from the UHS. This will help keep them "honest," the threat being that their customers (doctors, nurses, therapists, etc.) will drop out and become part of the UHS network if the cost of malpractice insurance is seriously hampering their efforts to make a decent living on the private side.

Our model will create malpractice review panels comprised of physicians and other healthcare professionals as needed, lawyers, public advocates, scientists involved in healthcare research, to make judgments concerning malpractice suits. This move will take responsibility for these decisions away from jury members who frequently lack the necessary knowledge and overview and who are vulnerable to manipulative lawyers.

These malpractice review panels will be established at the local level of the UHS network to adjudicate malpractice cases that arise in the local UHS sector—at community health centers and their satellites, at specialized clinics, and at general hospitals and research/teaching/medical hospitals. Panel members will be appointed by the Local UHS Board of Directors. The panels will have access to any evidence they require and will make decisions that are not binding. There will be one level of appeal, the state malpractice review panel established by the State UHS Board of Directors. When injured parties are not satisfied with the reward, they will have the right to find a lawyer and take the case to a traditional court.

The patients of practitioners in the local private sector can seek a judgment from the panel as well if so desired. As we have said, each panel will include physicians as well as other healthcare professionals on an as needed basis. These panel members will all work for the UHS if the suit is against a UHS employee, but will include private sector professionals if the suit is against a private sector employee.

Tort Reform

Our approach to healthcare will institute tort reform to cap the noneconomic portion of malpractice rewards that includes "pain and suffering." According to the literature, this portion in the United States, as we have said, typically comprises approximately 38 percent of the reward. The amount most often suggested for such a cap, as we have also said, is $250,000, which seems reasonable and is still higher than the level of reimbursement found in most European countries.

The rest of the reward is the economic portion based on how the medical error affects the claimant's ability to maintain and improve his or her standard of living and quality of life. The level of compensation, when the injury is judged by the malpractice review panel to not be the fault of the healthcare provider, will be set according to a predetermined schedule of damages. This schedule will be constructed by the previously mentioned group of experts brought together under the auspices of the National UHS Department of Healthcare Administration to set standards and define best practices. Their familiarity with the national standards and best practices they have previously defined will make it easier for them to decide on the best level of compensation for various injuries.

If it is decided that the injury occurred due to a healthcare provider's failure to meet a standard, the panel will decide the reward amount. It will also decide the provider's punishment. This can include a reprimand, a job suspension, a requirement that the provider receives further training, a requirement that the provider contribute part of the reward, or, in extreme cases, the loss of the provider's license to practice.

When the malpractice review panel's decision is accepted, the case will not involve a lawyer. As a result, there will be no court costs, not as much need for expert testimony, and not as much time spent on each case in that, for one thing, juries will not have to be selected and dealt with.

If the person who has filed the grievance is not satisfied with the panel's judgment, that person is free, as we have said, to hire a lawyer and go through the traditional court system. However, the cap for the noneconomic portion of the reward—$250,000—will remain in place. It can be assumed that fewer lawyers would be willing to represent clients pressing malpractice claims when caps that cut into their percentage have been instituted. It can also be assumed that victims would be less likely to hire a lawyer whose fee might take away as much as half of the reward.

Our model for dealing with malpractice allows healthcare providers who are found guilty, if, as punishment, they are forced to contribute part of the reward, to make periodic payment of damages so as not to suffer bankruptcy. The malpractice review panel will decide the schedule of payments.

Our model also takes into account payments for treatment of the involved injury that are received from other sources, such as medical insurance or disability insurance. Currently, the Collateral Source Rule prohibits those being judged from introducing evidence that the plaintiff is receiving such payment. The argument is that the involved evidence might negatively affect the jury's decision concerning a financial reward. However, because we are no longer dealing with juries, because the payment schedule for economic damages when the healthcare provider has been found not to be at fault is already set, because we have capped noneconomic damages, in our model, this information will be taken into account before judgment is passed.

Keeping Watch

Finally, our model for dealing with malpractice is designed to encourage peer review. Normally, the practice of peer review tends to be pretty much of a farce. It is a farce when lawyers are made responsible for monitoring and correcting the behavior of lawyers, when accountants are supposed to monitor the behavior of accountants, when corporate CEO's who sit on each other's boards are put in charge of keeping watch over the ethical behavior of their peers. The "old boy" mentality, the reward system that shapes such situations, usually pushes them in the other direction.

While almost half of our states require the reporting of medical errors and adverse events, it is estimated that a majority of malpractice instances remain hidden. Lawyers are not allowed to roam the halls of hospitals, and staff members are frequently afraid of retribution if they report something they have seen. There is little reward for bringing to light an incidence of malpractice. Careers are tarnished. The organization's reputation is tarnished. Regulator bodies descend with a host of new requirements. Potential patients stay away.

Organizations at both the federal and state level exist to keep track of the number of medical errors committed, to investigate, and sometimes to discipline. The foremost of these is the State Medical Board. Most of the board's work, however, is done on a case-by-case basis. Thus, the board is usually too busy dealing with individual cases and too busy cleaning up individual messes to address the underlying causes of malpractice.

In our model, once again, the malpractice issues and, more specifically, the emphasis on peer review that can greatly diminish the amount of malpractice occurring, do not stand alone, but are interconnected and dependent to a large degree on other parts of the model. Open communication and transparency are, of course, important. Training is also extremely important. But, the greatest deterrent to malpractice that we have proposed is our unique reward system.

Quite simply, in our model, physicians are no longer rewarded according to the number of patients treated. In our model, the rest of the professional staff is not dependent simply on salary. Rather, in our model, everybody's reward is based on how healthy the team keeps its client population.

In the traditional setting, if a physician or another professional makes an error, it affects only the culprit along with the culprit's insurance company unless the victim decides to sue the organization as well. Even if the organization is sued, however, few other staff are affected. They still receive their salaries.

In our model, if a medical error is made and a malpractice suit is instituted, it is almost certain that word will get out and that other patients served by the team will start thinking about finding a different team to care for them. People want to keep track of the history of their attending physician.

If patients start dropping off a team's roll, everybody on that team will suffer because the amount earned through bonuses will decrease. Thus, all employees will be encouraged to constantly review the work of their peers. Thus, professionals will be more willing to seek advice concerning decisions of which they are not sure. Thus, when an error does occur, all employees will be more eager to make sure that the same error does not occur again.

Peer review will become an important part of everyday procedure for everybody, not by order, but as a result of reward-based incentive.

SO, THAT'S IT...

So, now the reader has the DeSales Group's design of what it considers to be an ideal healthcare system for the United States. This design is based on the premise that *comprehensive healthcare should be a right, not a privilege.* The driving force behind our decision is not altruism so much as common sense. If we are going to remain competitive on the world economic stage, we need to effectively utilize the potential of our citizens, and without adequate healthcare, that potential will not be realized or utilized.

Our model contains parts borrowed from other countries with systems considered superior to ours. It takes national, state, and local politics out of healthcare. It reorganizes the healthcare domain in a sensible manner that emphasizes integration. It includes incentives for prevention. It gets rid of most of the competition currently found between delivery systems. It gets rid of the profit motive that drives the price of services upward. It greatly reduces the role of insurance companies and lawyers, making the system more cost effective. It includes an information system that links facilities across the country, provides information on an as-needed basis, and encourages comprehensive research. It allows affordable training so that we can deal with predicted shortages. It relieves healthcare providers of the financial burden imposed by malpractice insurance and suits.

All of these things are being done in other countries. Our model, however, also includes something we believe is new, something that supports all of the above and is probably the model's core. *That is, our reward system allows providers to improve their salaries by making their services unnecessary, while, at the same time, patients can benefit financially by staying healthy. The final result being that the overall cost of healthcare to our nation decreases.*

Does this sound too good to be true? Well, it's not, but the reward system is just one piece of the puzzle. Without the others, it will not produce the desired results. Obviously, our culture needs to change for such a model to succeed; obviously, such change is going to be difficult, many of those with a stake in the current approach fighting anything new, throwing rocks at anything that moves, no matter how beneficial it might be.

The desired change will take time, and patience. But now that we have a comprehensive model, we at least have a target to aim for. How do we get there from here? How do we get to where we want to be ideally from where we are now? I'm not sure. We'll leave that up to you. Or, maybe it will be the subject of another book: how to deliver the healthcare system that we all want, we all deserve. We'll see.

Anyway, now that we have successfully put together what we wanted to offer, it's time to rest. So, for the DeSales group, I say, I hope that our contribution will be of use, and take care ...

REFERENCES

1. Medical Malpractice Reform, *Policy, Politics, & Nursing Practice*, 4 (3), August 2003.
2. Addressing the Medical Malpractice Insurance Crisis, *NGA Center for Best Practices*, December 5, 2002, p. 6.
3. Medical Malpractice, p.5: http://wikipedia.org/wiki/Medical_malpractice (accessed February 14, 2009).
4. Rising Doctors' Premiums Not Due to Lawsuit Awards, Liz Kowalczyk, *Boston Globe*, June 1, 2005.
5. *Addressing the Medical Malpractice Insurance Crisis*, NGA Center for Best Practices, Washington, D.C., December 5, 2002, p. 2.
6. Trends in 2001 Rates for Physicians' Medical Professional Liability Insurance, *Medical Liability Monitor*, 26 (10), October 2001.
7. Medical Malpractice Reform, *Policy, Politics, and Nursing Practice*, 4 (3), August 2003.
8. Medical Malpractice, *Insurance Information Institute: The Topic*, January 2009, p. 2.
9. Law and Medicine: Sweden, Nicholas Beaudrot, *Electoral Math*, April 2005, pp. 1–2.
10. Law and Medicine: United Kingdom, Nicholas Beaudrot, *Electoral Math*, April 2005, pp. 6–7.
11. Medical Malpractice and Legal Resolution Systems in Japan, Kazue Nakajima, Catherine Keyes, Tatsuo Kuroyanagi, Kozo Tatara, *JAMA*, 285, 2001, 1632–1640.

Bibliography

A Profile of Medicare: Chartbook 1998, U.S. Health Care Financing Administration, Washington D.C., May 1998.

Ackoff, Russell L., *Redesigning the Future: A Systems Approach to Societal Problems*, New York: John Wiley & Sons, 1960.

Addressing the Medical Malpractice Insurance Crisis, NGA Center for Best Practices, Washington, D.C., December 5, 2002.

Allio, Robert J., Ackoff, Russell L., Iconoclastic Management Authority, Advocates a "Systemic" Approach to Innovation, *Strategy and Leadership*, 31, 2003.

Bankauskaite, V., Saltman, R.B., Vrangback, K., The Role of Decentralization of European Health Care Systems, *Report to IPPR, European Observatory of Health Systems and Policies and Department of Political Science*, University of Copenhagen, February 2004.

Basic Questions about Universal Health Care Insurance for All: http://www.hcforall.org (accessed July 29, 2008).

Bates, D., Ebell, M., Gottlieb, E., Zapp, J., Mullins, H.C., A Proposal for Electronic Medical Records in U.S. Primary Care. *The Journal of the American Medical Informatics Association*, January 2003.

Beaudrot, Nicholas, Law and Medicine: Sweden, *Electoral Math*, April 2005.

Brewin, Bob, UK Begins $4.7B Electronic Patient Records Project, *Bio-IT World*, (2003): http://www.bioitworld.com/new/ (accessed October 21, 2004).

Bringing Pass/Fail to Preclinical Curricula, *American Medical Student Association*. (2003): http://www.amsa.org/meded/passfail.cfm (accessed November 15, 2003).

Brown, Chris, Private Sector Health Care Leads the Way, *Mises Daily*, December 3, 2008: http://mises.org/story/3233 (accessed February 5, 2009).

Brown, Lawrence D., The Amazing, Noncollapsing U.S Health Care System: Is Reform at Hand? *New England Journal of Medicine*, 358 (4):325–327, January 21, 2008.

Canadian Healthcare Technology: http://www.canhealth.com (accessed February 2004).

Chua, Kao-Ping, Overview of the U.S. Health Care System, American Medical Student Association (AMSA) Jack Rutledge Fellow, February 10, 2006.

David M. Studdert, Michelle M. Mello, Atul A. Gawande, Tejal K. Gandhi, Allen Kachalia, Catherine Yoon, Ann Louise Puopolo, and Troyen A. Brennan, Claims, Errors, and Compensation Payments in Medical Malpractice Litigation, *New England Journal of Medicine*, 354 (2024–2033): 332–341, May 11, 2006.

Clinton Offers Universal Health Care Plan, *Associated Press*, Monday, September 17, 2007.

Conrad, Peter, *The Sociology of Health and Illness: Critical Perspectives*, New York: Worth Publishers, 2001.

Cooper, E., Taylor, L., Comparing Health Care Systems: What Makes Sense for the U.S.? *Good Medicine*, Fall, 1994.

Cooper, Robert, Medical Schools and Their Applicants: An Analysis, *Medical Affairs*, 22 (4), 2003.

Country Report: Medical Education in France, *Medical Education*, 41, (3), March 2007.

Creating a New National Workforce for Internal Medicine, Position paper, American College of Physicians, Philadelphia, 2006.

Cross, Michael, Britain's Healthcare System Gets a Jumpstart, *Healthcare Informatics: International*, (2000): http://www.healthcareinformatics.com/issues/2000/05_00/international.htm (accessed October 16, 2004).

Data on national health and nutrition examination survey 2006. National Institute of Environmental Health Sciences, National Institutes of Health, Bethesda, Maryland. 146 (6): 416–420, September 16, 2008.

Duriez, Marc, The French Health Care System: Organization and Functioning, Paris: *CREDES*, 1994.

Dutton, Paul, France's Model Healthcare System, *The Boston Globe*, August 11, 2007.

European Physicians, Especially in Sweden, Netherlands and Denmark, Lead U.S. in Use of Electronic Medical Records, *Harris Interactive, Healthcare Research* 2, (16), (2002): http://www.harrisinteractive.com (accessed October 23, 2004).

Experts: U.S. Health Care System Wastes Millions, *The Washington Post*, Washington, D.C., December 1, 2008.

Fahrenthold, David, Mass. Bill Requires Health Coverage, *The Washington Post*, April 5, 2006.

France's Model Healthcare System, *The Boston Globe*, August 11, 2007.

Goldman, David, Obama's Big Idea: Digital Health Records," *CNNMoney*: http://money.cnn.com/2009/01/12/technology/stimulus_health_care/ (accessed January 12, 2009).

Goldsmith, J., *Digital Medicine*, Chicago: Health Administration Press, 2003.

Grant, Sue, Healthcare in Germany, *Medhunters Magazine*, Spring, 2003.

Health Care around the World: An Introduction, *Health Care Economist*, April 14, 2008.

Health Information Technology: Can HIT Lower Costs and Improve Quality? *Rand Health*, 2005.

Health Level Seven: Answering the Country's Need for a National Health Information Infrastructure, *IBM*, 2003: http://www.ibm.com/mediumbusiness/resources/white-papers/whitepaper.jsp?contentId=8564 (accessed February 1, 2004).

Health Systems Resources, *World Health Statistics 2008: Global Health Indicators*, World Health Organization, Geneva, 2008.

Italy's Public Health-Care System Is Doing Poorly, *The New York Times*, January 1, 2009.

Jolly, Paul, Medical School Tuition and Young Physicians' Indebtedness, *Health Affairs: The Policy Journal of the Health Sphere*, 24 (2), 2005.

Nakajima, K., Keyes, C., Kuroyanagi, T., Tatara, K., Medical Malpractice and Legal Resolution Systems in Japan, *JAMA*, 285, 2001, 1632–1640.

Kowalczyk, Liz, Rising Doctors' Premiums Not Due to Lawsuit Awards, *The Boston Globe*, June 1, 2005.

Local Government in Sweden: Organization, Activities and Finance, *The Ministry of Finance*: http://www.finans.regeringen.se (accessed December 5, 2004).

Lomax, R.C., Swedish Healthcare Structure, *University of South Carolina/Columbia*, December 1, 2004.

Maio, V., Mansoli, L., The Italian Health Care System: W.H.O. Ranking versus Public Perception, *P&T*, 27 (6), 2002.

McDonald, F., West, C., Popkave, C., Kolars, J., Educational Debt and Reported Career Plans amongst Internal Medicine Residents, *Academia and Clinic: Annals of Internal Medicine*, 2008.

Medical Malpractice Insurance. Insurance Information Institute. Insurance Issues Series 1 (1), June 2003.

Medical Malpractice: http://wikipedia.org/wiki/Medical_malpractice (accessed February 14, 2009).

Medical Malpractice Reform, *Policy, Politics, and Nursing Practice*, 4 (3), August 2003.

Monteagudo, Jose Luis, eHealth in Spain: Current Situation and Major Trends, Abstract; eHealth 2003–Telematics in Healthcare, National Strategies in Centralised and Federal State Systems, National and International Congress, Dresden, Germany (October 21–23, 2003): http://www.spainhealthcare.com (accessed October 16, 2004).

Mythbuster: The Seven Most Important Things to Know about Medical Malpractice, New York: Center for Justice and Democracy, February 10, 2004, p. 3.

Obama Healthcare Plan Relies on the Evidence, *Reuters News Service*, Thursday, February 26, 2009.

Ostergaard, H.T., Ostergaard, D., Lippert, A., Implementation of Team Training in Medical Education in Denmark, *Quality of Health Care*, 13 (Suppl. 1), 2004.

Pharmaceutical Company Expenses: Cost of Sales, Marketing, R&D Compared: http://www.cptech.org/ip/health/econ/allocation.html (accessed March 16, 2009).

Pharmaceutical Drug Companies Killing Middle America Legally While Robbing You Blind: http://www.betterbodyjournal.com (accessed March 15, 2009).

Physicians Are Not Invincible, *Southern Medical Journal*, 93 (10), 2000.

Physicians for a National Health Program: http://www,pnhp.org (accessed February 2009).

President Obama's Plan Vastly Expands American Health Care, *The Washington Post*, February 26, 2009.

Reforming Dysfunctional Payment Policies, underdraft by the Medical Services Committee of the American College of Physicians, Philadelphia, 2009.

Reinhardt, Uwe E., Germany's Health Care System: It's Not the American Way, *Health Affairs*, Fall, 1994.

Reinhardt, Uwe E., Why Does U.S. Health Care Cost So Much? *Economix, Explaining the Science of Everyday Life*, December 12, 2008.

Rodwin, V., The Health Care System under French National Insurance: Lessons for Health Reform in the United States, *American Journal of Public Health*, 93 (1), January 2003.

Romney, Mitt, Health Care for Everyone? *The Wall Street Journal*, Tuesday, April 11, 2006.

Roth, William F., Yes, Tests Still Rule, *American School Board Journal*, 192 (5): May 2005, 57–58.

Roth, William F., *Ethics in the Workplace: A Systems Perspective*, Upper Saddle River, N.J.: Pearson Prentice Hall, 2005.

Roth, W., Ryder, J., Voehl, F. *Problem Solving for Results*, Delray Beach, FL: St. Lucie Press, 1996.

Sakjeverm, A., A Paperless Healthcare System? *BusinessWeek*, (2004): http://www.Businessweek. com/technology/content/jul2004/tc2004077 8164_tc_171.htm (accessed July 7, 2004).

Schroeder, Steven, The Clinton Health Care Plan: Fundamental or Incremental Reform? *Annals of Internal Medicine*, 119 (9), November 1, 1993.

Shaw, Andy, Calgary Health Region Creates a Leading Edge Chronic Care System, *Canadian Healthcare Technology*: http://www.canhealth.com (accessed January 2, 2005).

Sweden's Healthcare/IT Advances-Lessons Learned, *ITAC Healthcare Videoconference Simulcast*: http://www.itac.ca/Health/PastEvents/ITACSwedensHealthcare.htm (accessed October 23, 2004).

The French Health Care System: A Brief Overview, *CREDES*, October 2001.

The French Lesson in Health Care, *BusinessWeek*, July 9, 2007.

The Italian Health Care System: WHO Ranking versus Public Perception, *P&T*, 27 (6), 2002.

The Italian National Health System: http://www.globalcitizenship.at/workspace/att/file98984926.doc (accessed February 10, 2009).

The Medical Malpractice Insurance Crisis: Opportunity for State Action, Princeton, NJ: The Robert Wood Johnson Foundation, July 2002.

The World Health Report 2000—Health Systems: Improving Performance, Geneva: World Health Organization, 2000.

To Err Is Human: Building a Safer Health System, Institute of Medicine, Washington, D.C.: National Academy Press, 1999.

Trends in 2001 Rates for Physicians' Medical Professional Liability Insurance, *Medical Liability Monitor*, 26 (10), October 2001.

Trends in Health Telematics in the European Union. *EHTO Enterprise, SA*, 1996: http://www.ehto.org/ht_projects/trends/uk.html (accessed October 15, 2004).

Waiting Your Turn: Hospital Waiting Lists in Canada, *Fraser Institute's 14th Annual Edition*, Vancouver, BC, 2004.

Wray, Richard, Life-saving Research Missing Out in Health Spending, *The Guardian Unlimited*, (2004): http://www.guardian.co.uk/business/story/ (accessed October 14, 2004).

Written Testimony for the Senate Finance Committee Hearing on International Trade and Pharmaceuticals," *Families USA*, April 27, 2004.

About the Author

William F. Roth, PhD, is currently a professor at Kutztown University in Pennsylvania, where he teaches courses in strategic planning, organization design, and management theory. Previously he taught for sixteen years at DeSales University (Center Valley, Pennsylvania), where most of the research for this book was completed.

Dr. Roth earned his PhD in social systems sciences at The Wharton School, his master's degree in social work at the University of Pennsylvania, and his bachelor's degree in economic geography at Dartmouth College. As a consultant, Dr. Roth has worked on design and regional planning projects in Saudi Arabia, Iran, Mexico, and several locations in the United States. Previously, he spent five years with the Poverty Program and the Civil Rights Movement in the Deep South. In addition to this book, Dr. Roth has authored five others, as well as more than fifty articles in a wide range of professional journals. He also writes fiction and has published several prize-winning short stories.

Index